I am grateful to God for everything!

Robert de Paula
2024

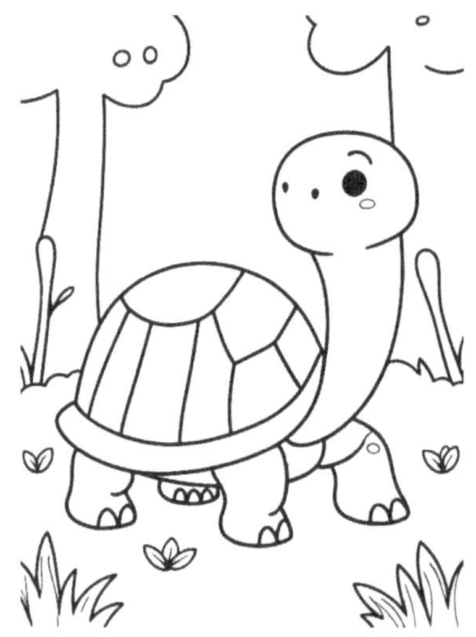

This Book Belongs to:

____

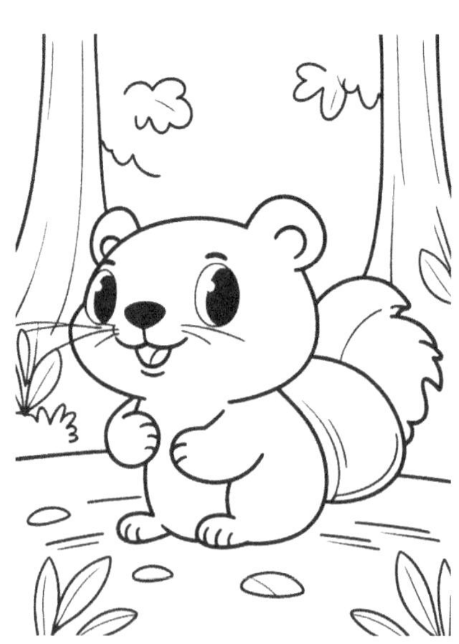

Test Color Page

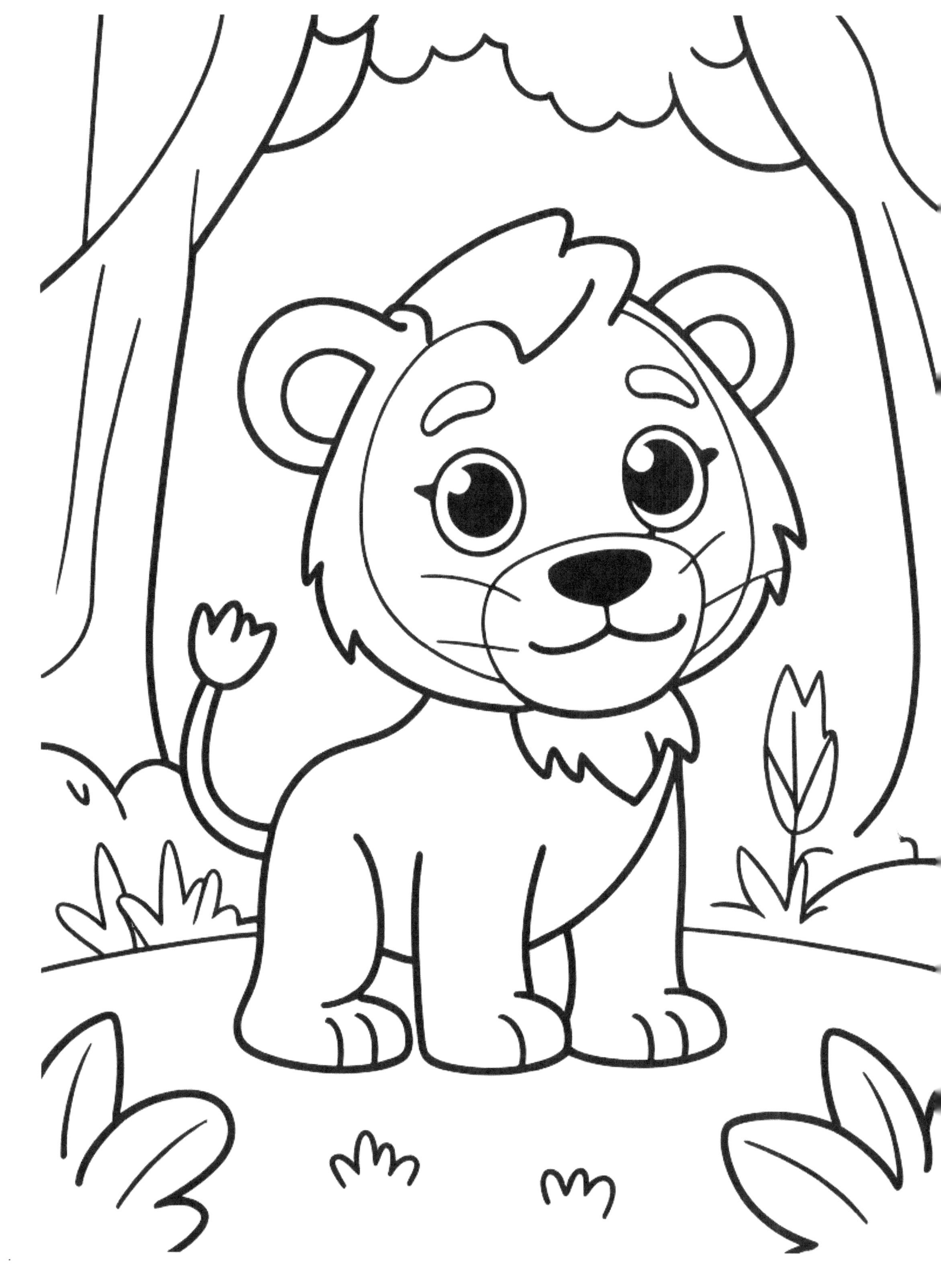

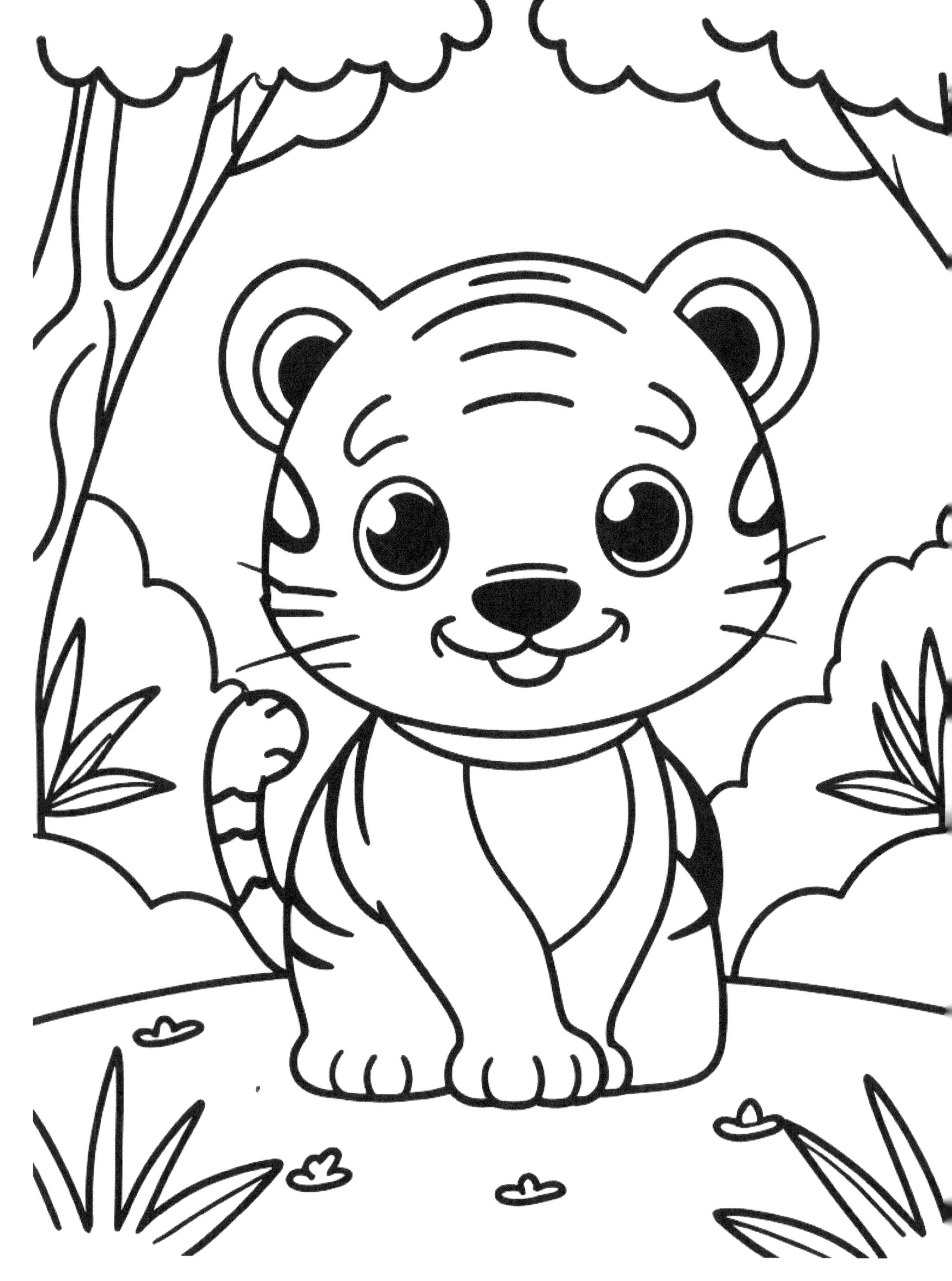

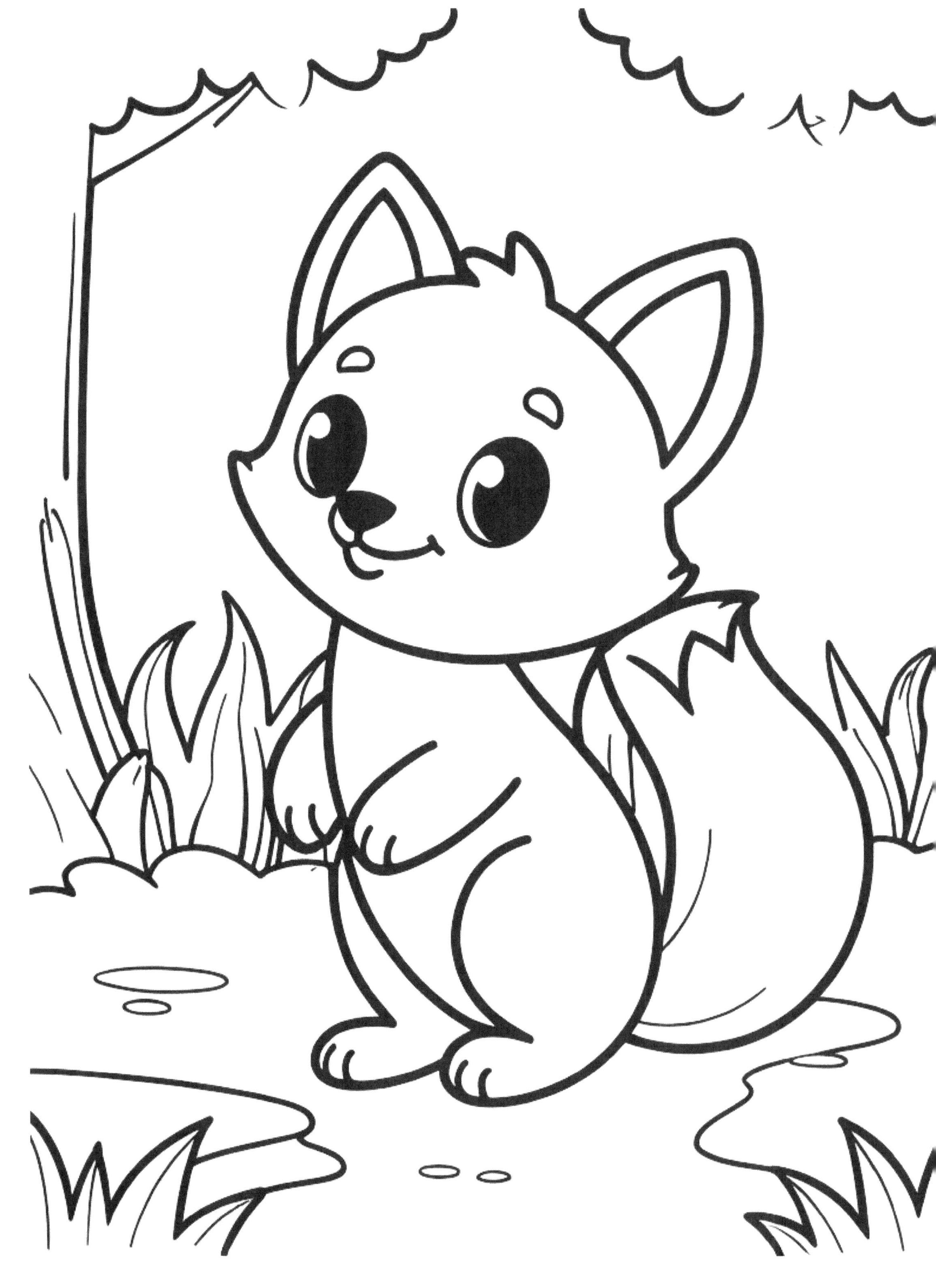

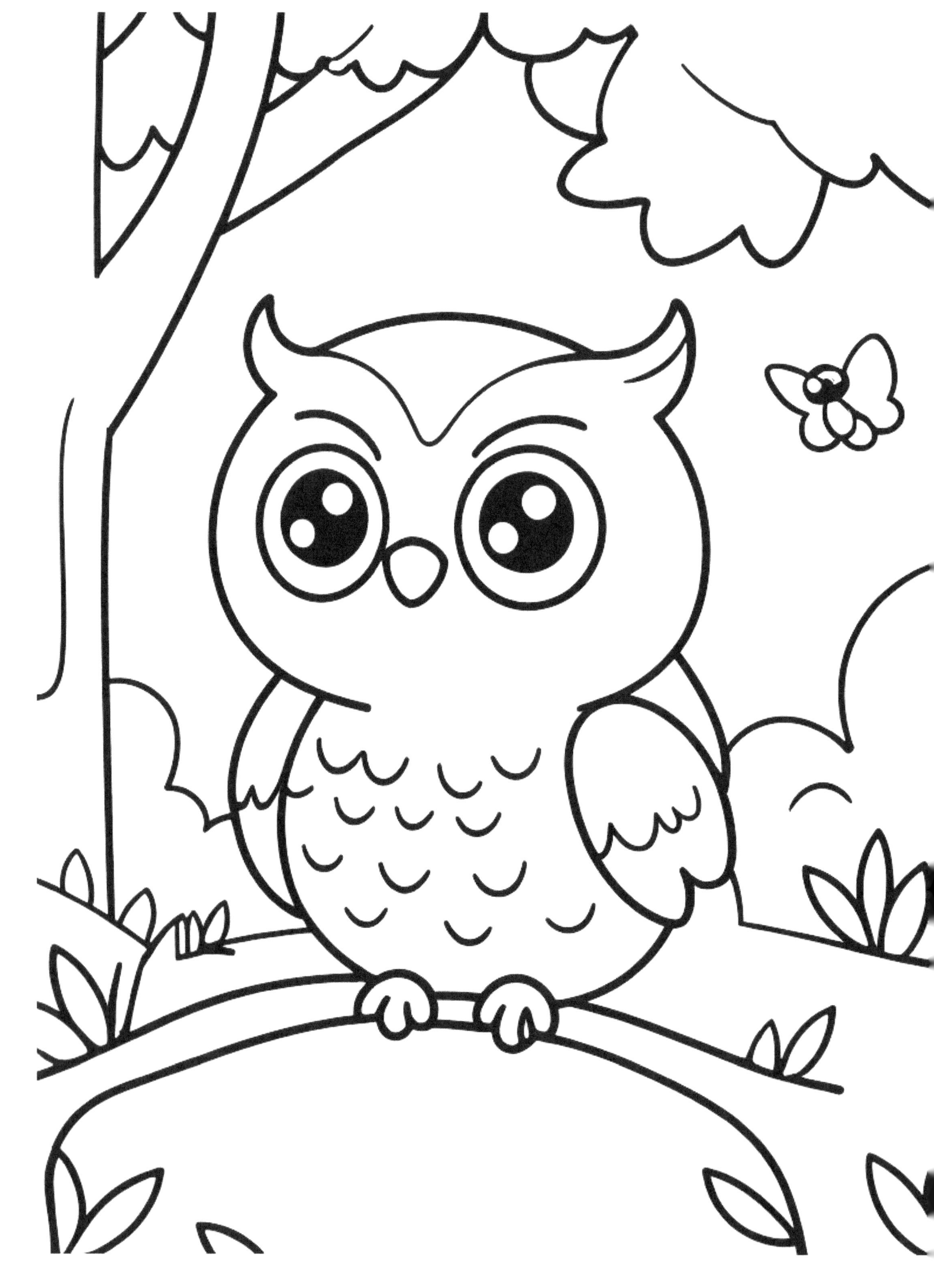

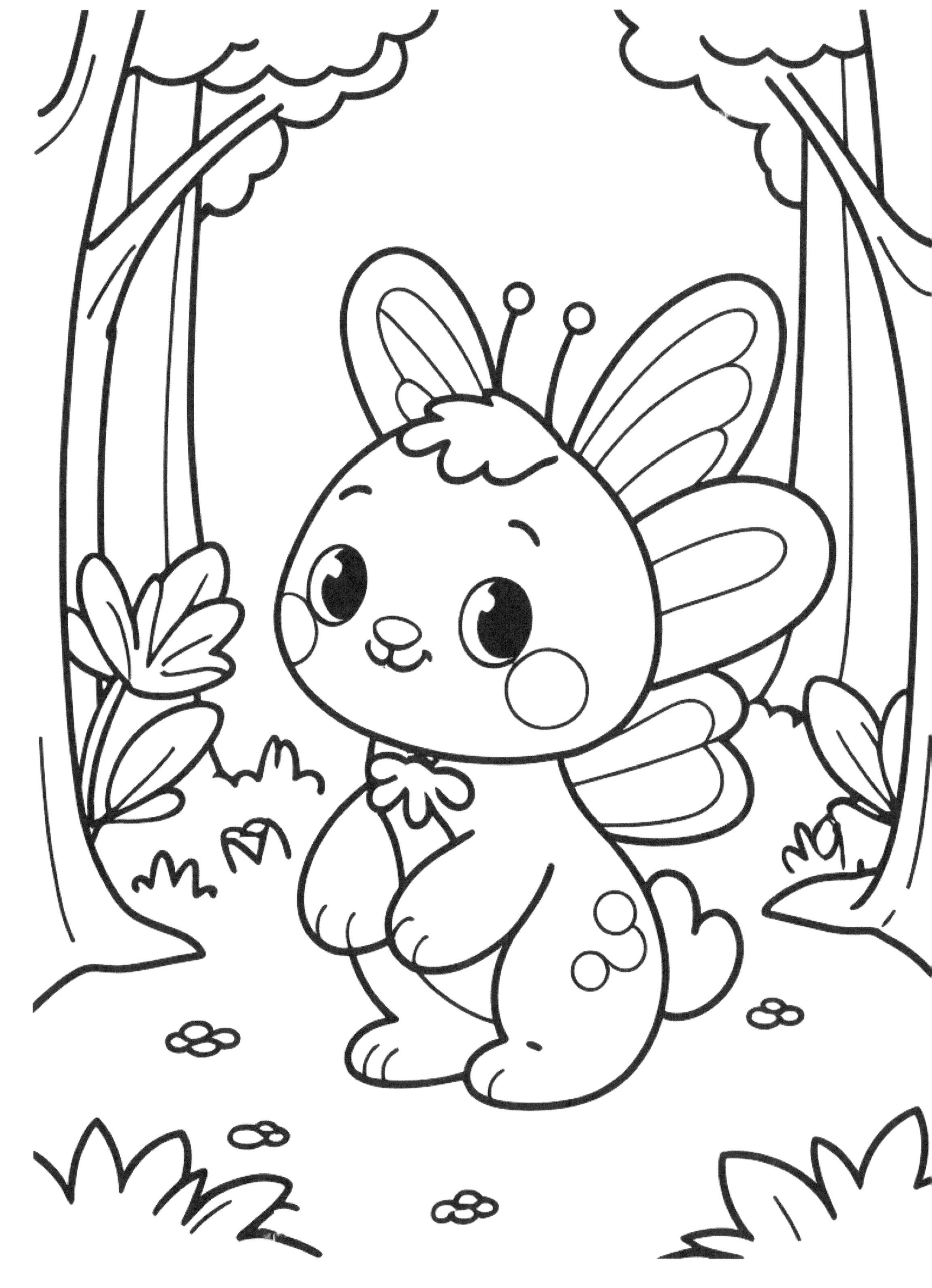

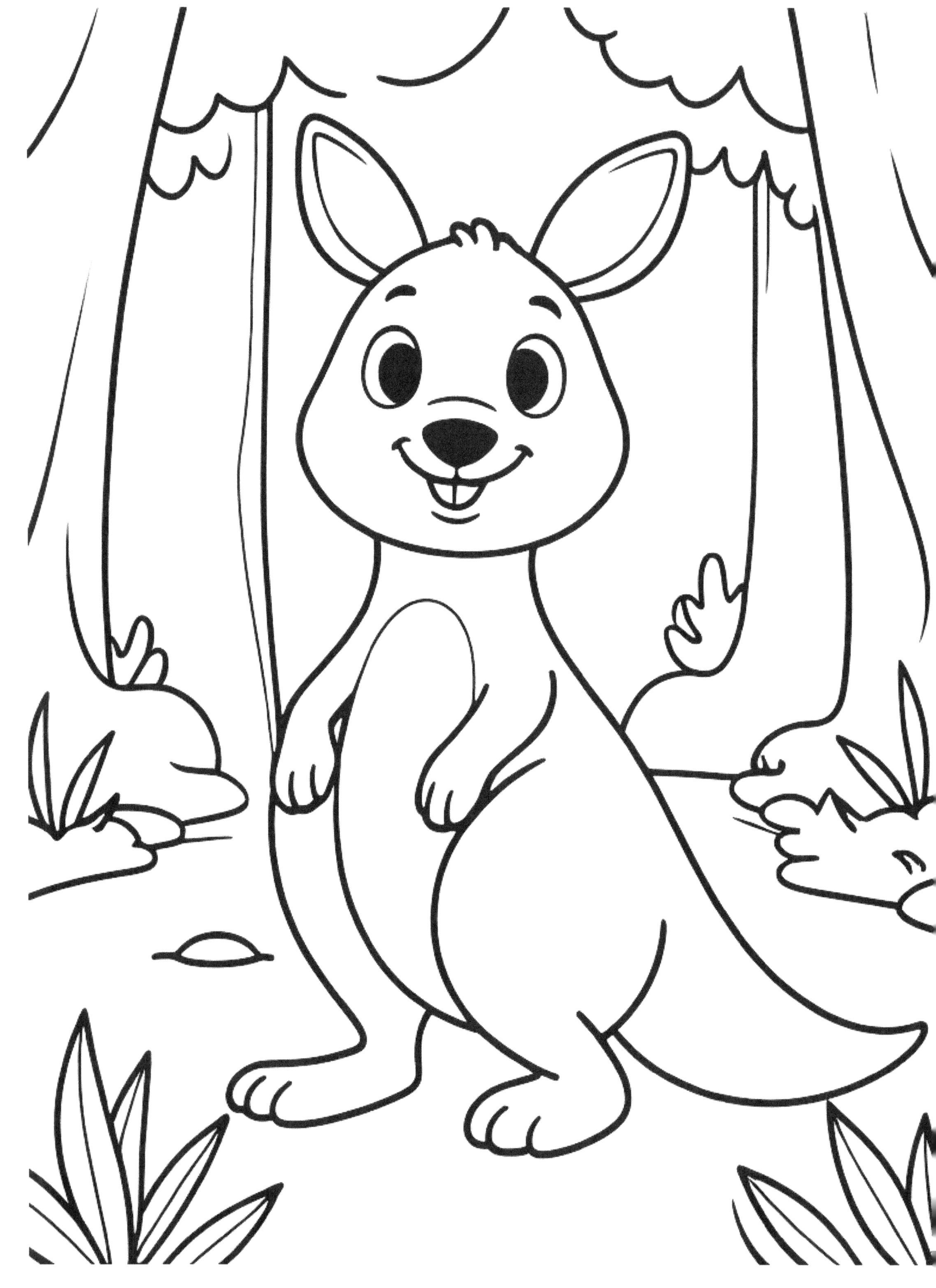

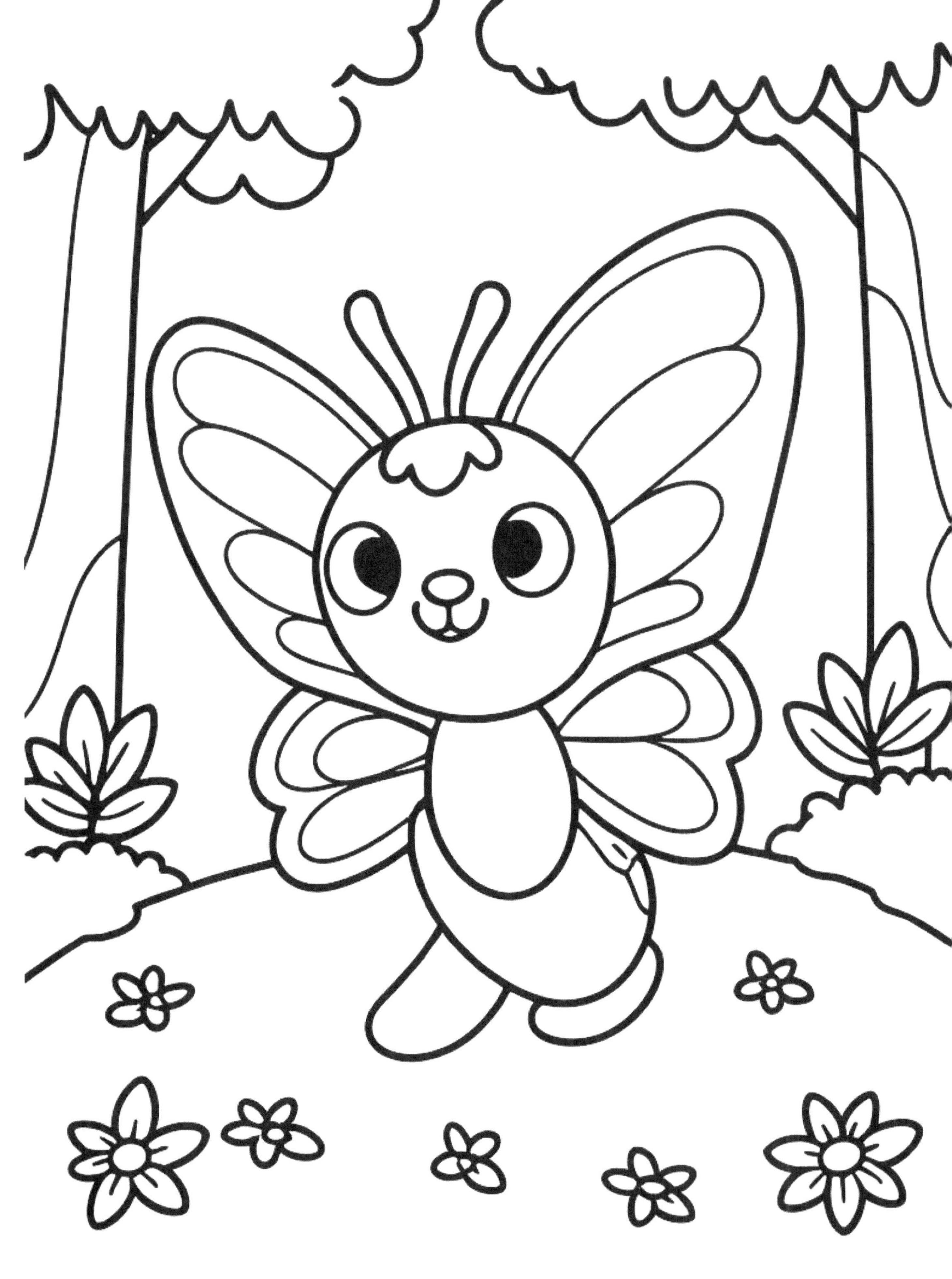

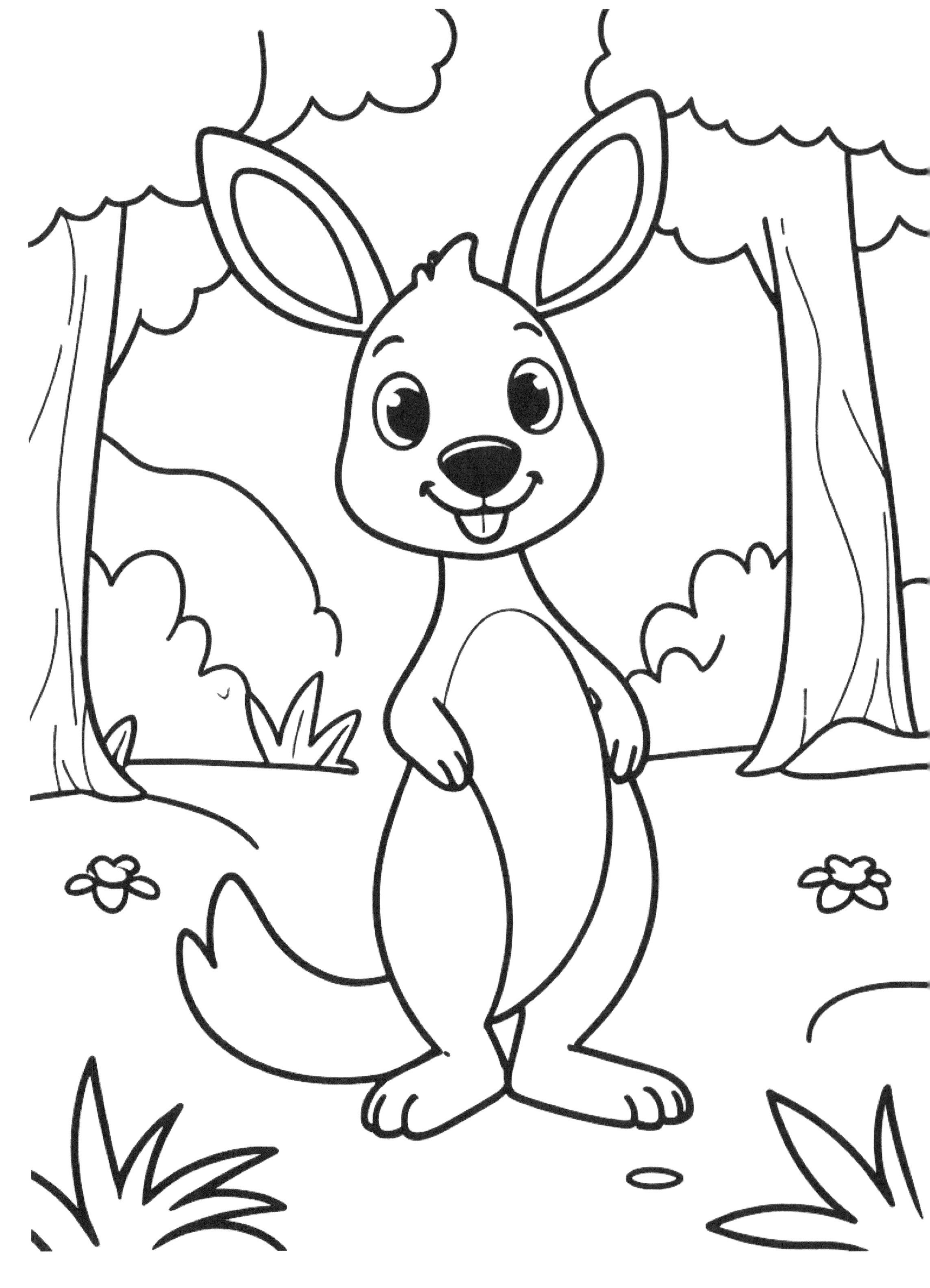

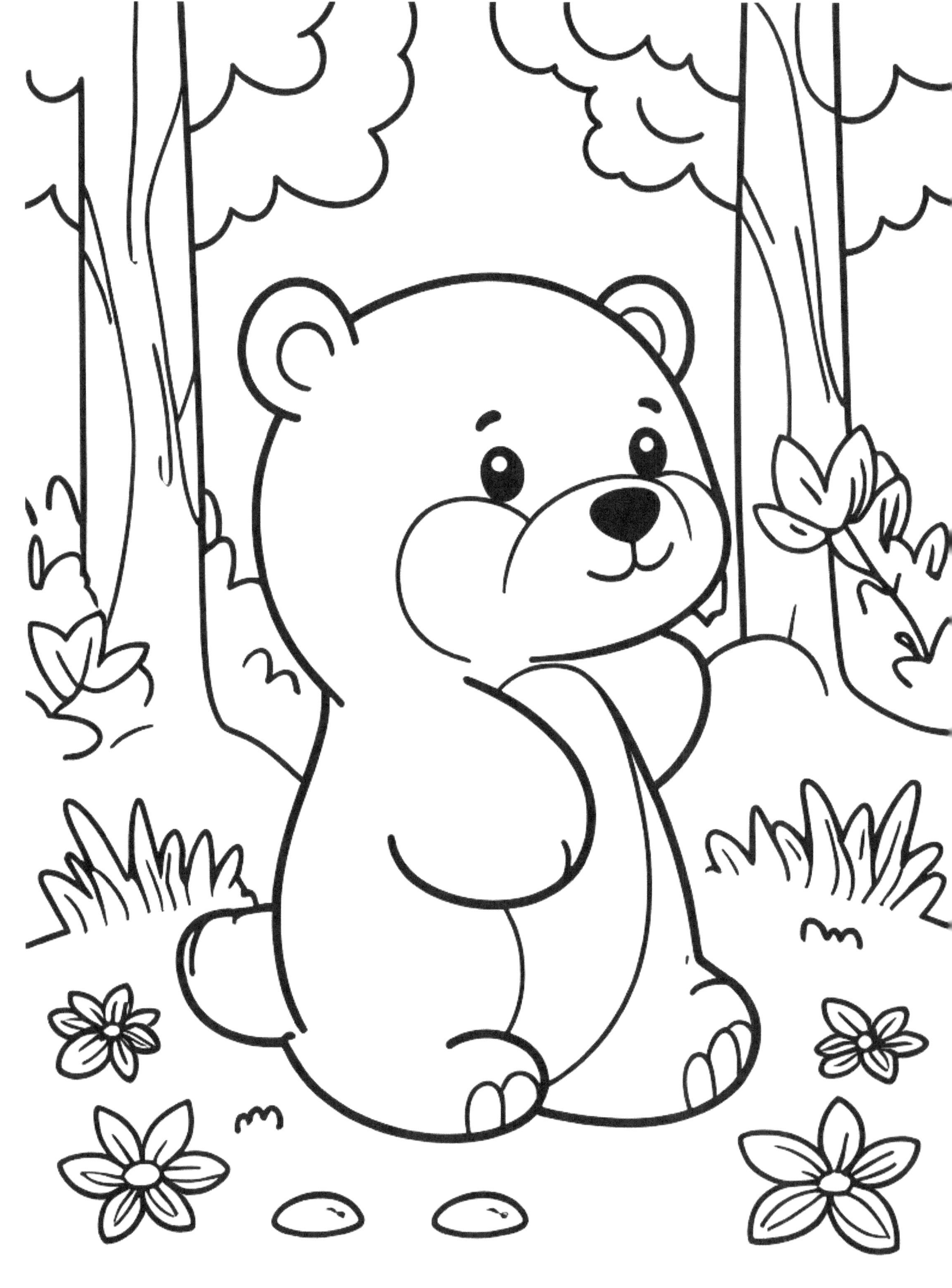

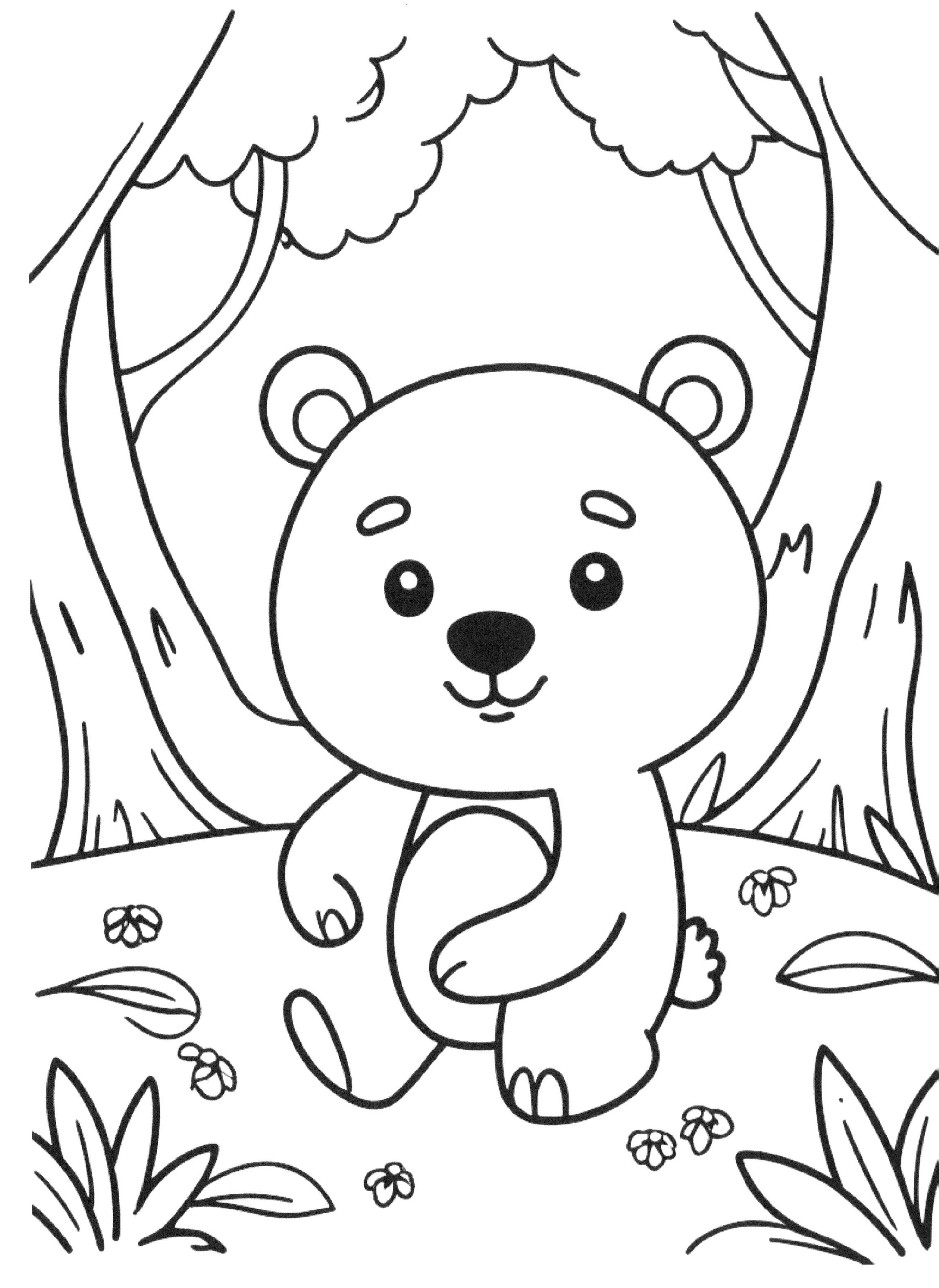

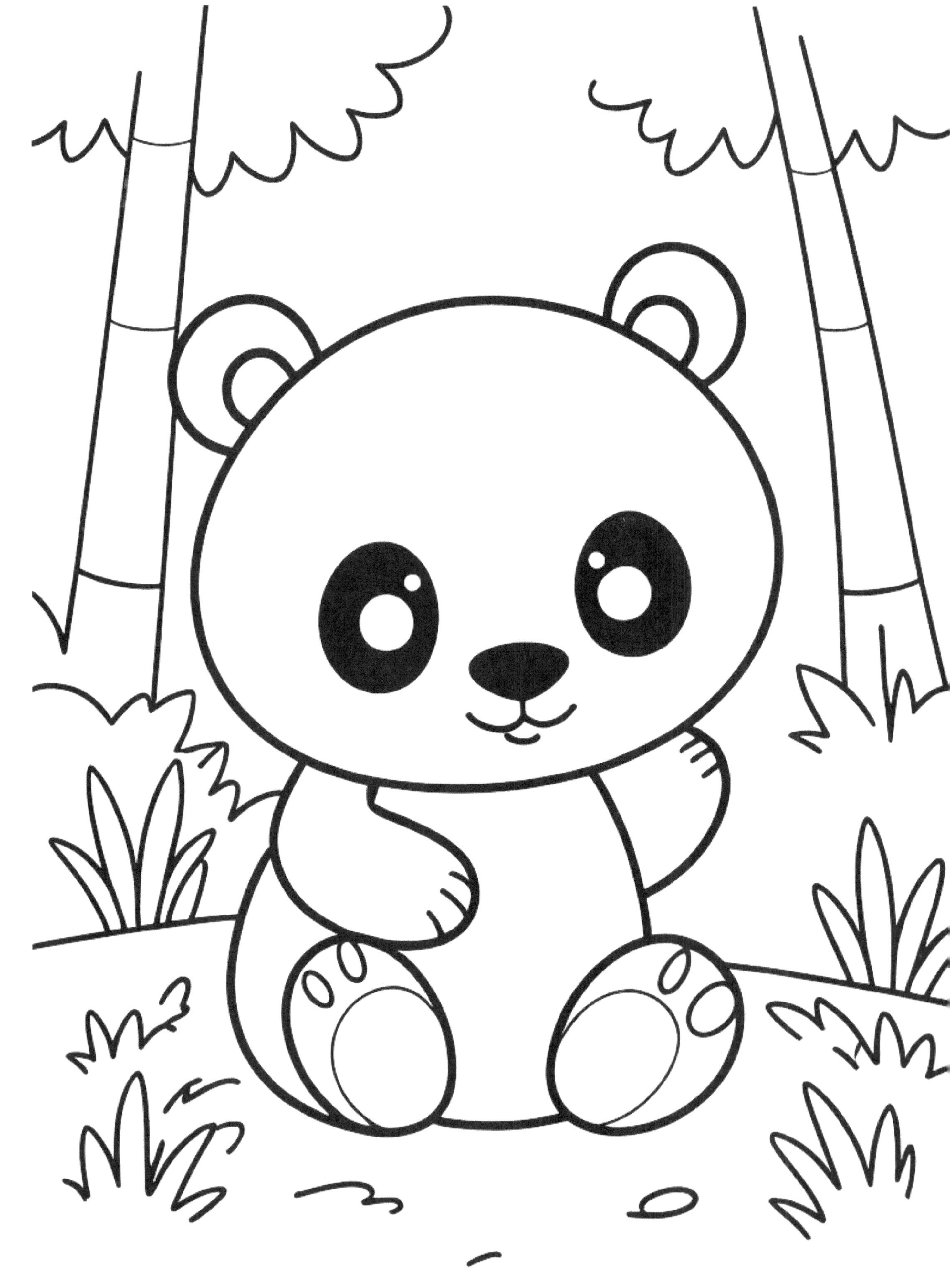

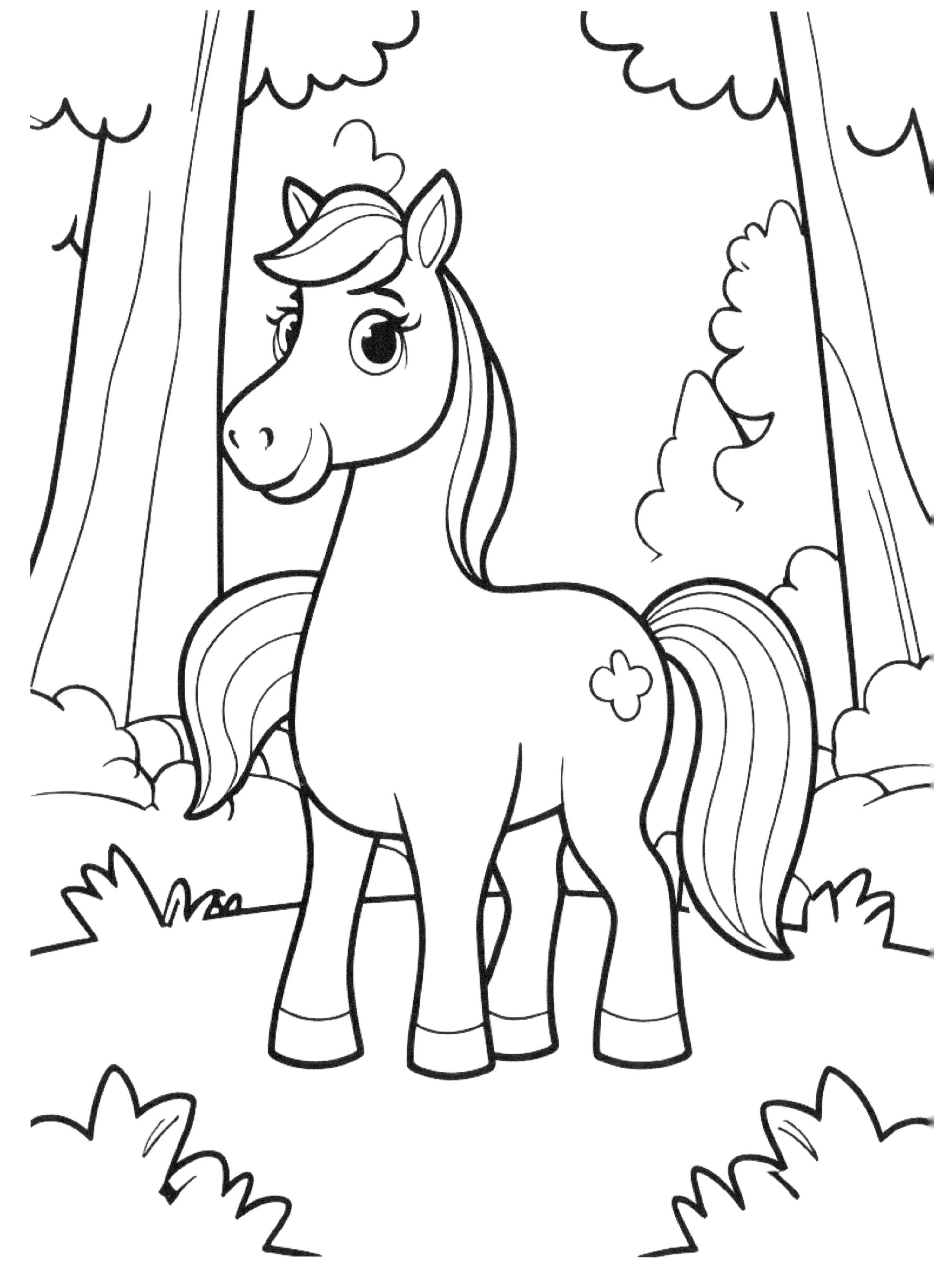

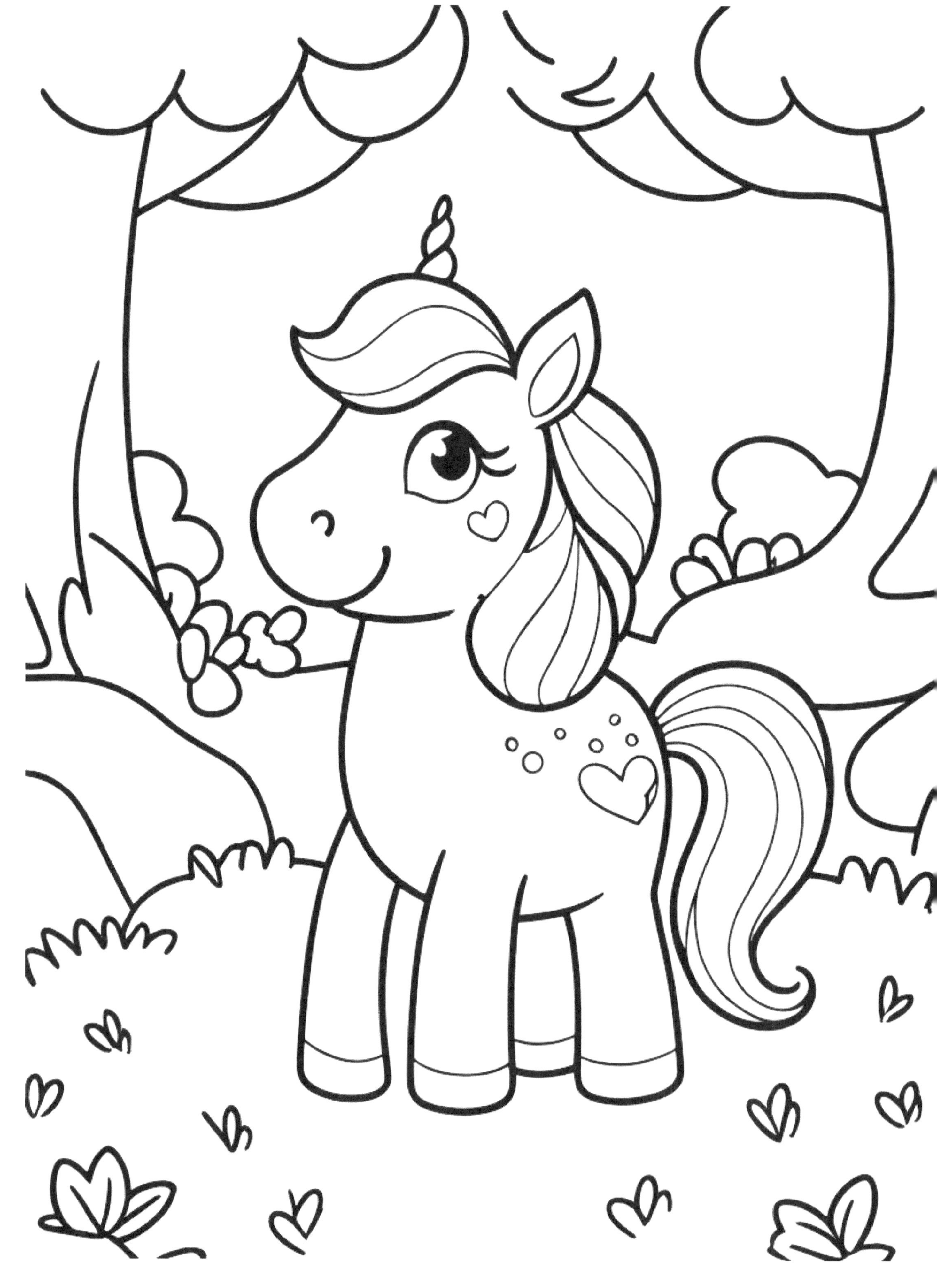

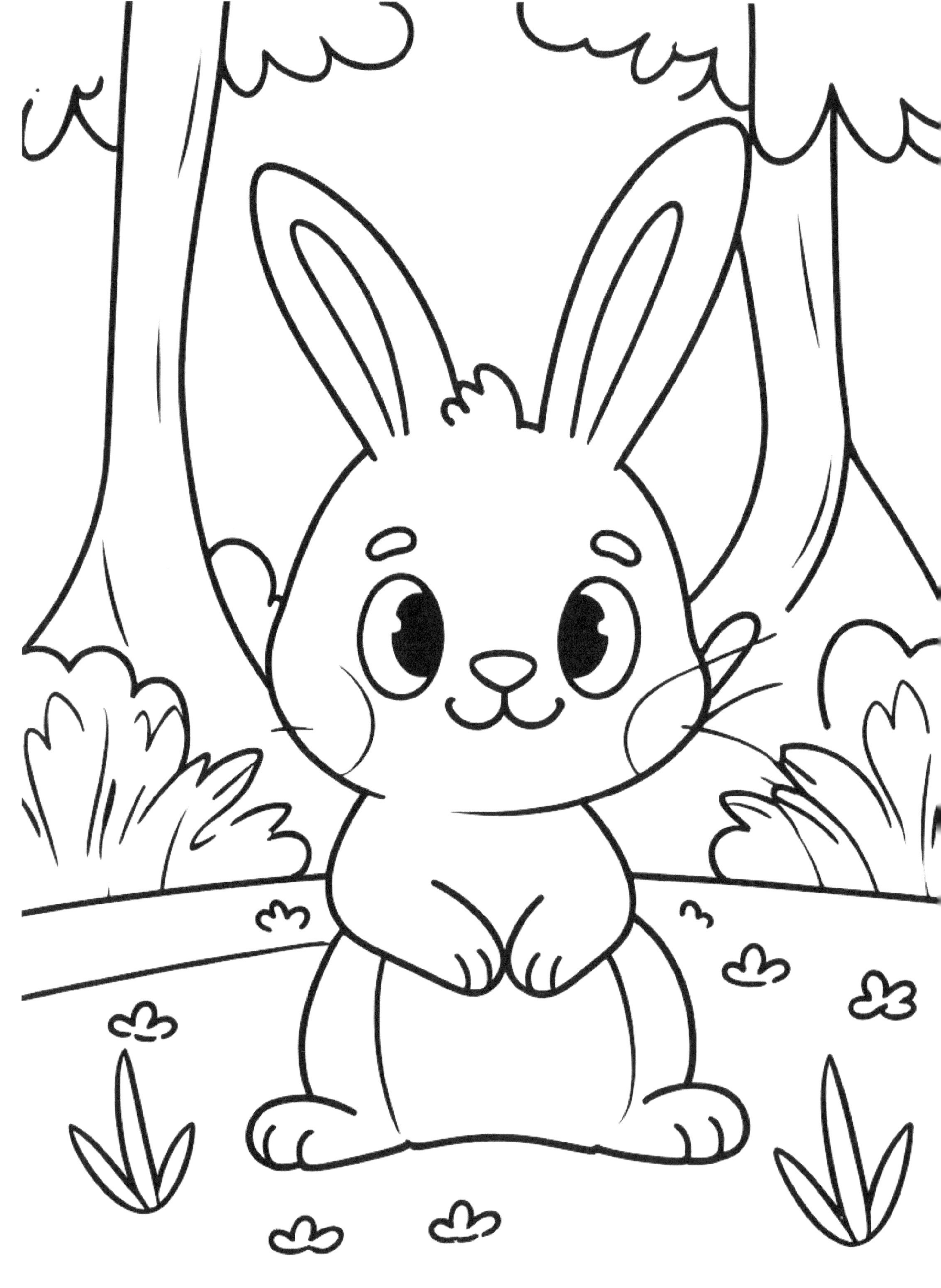

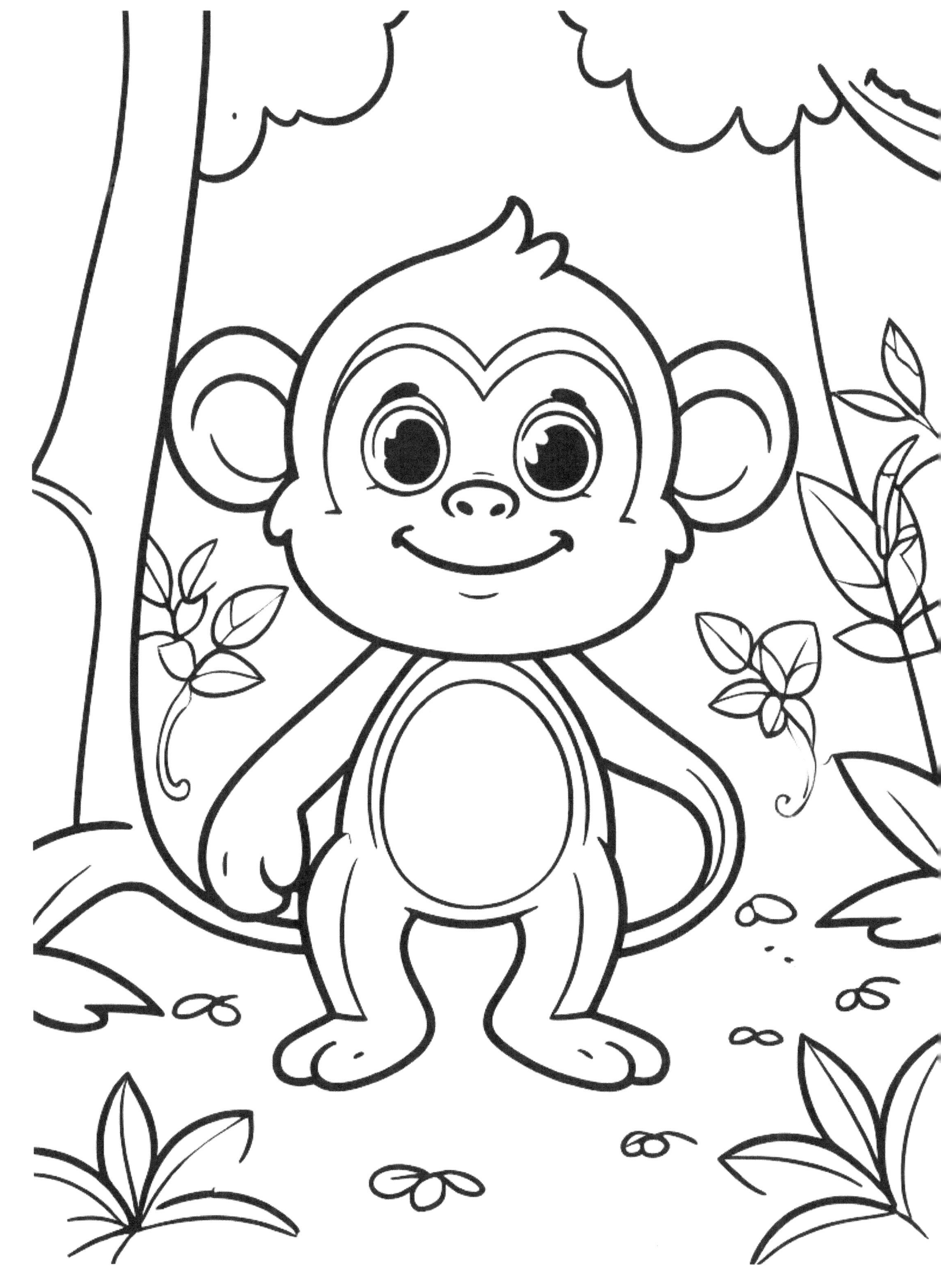

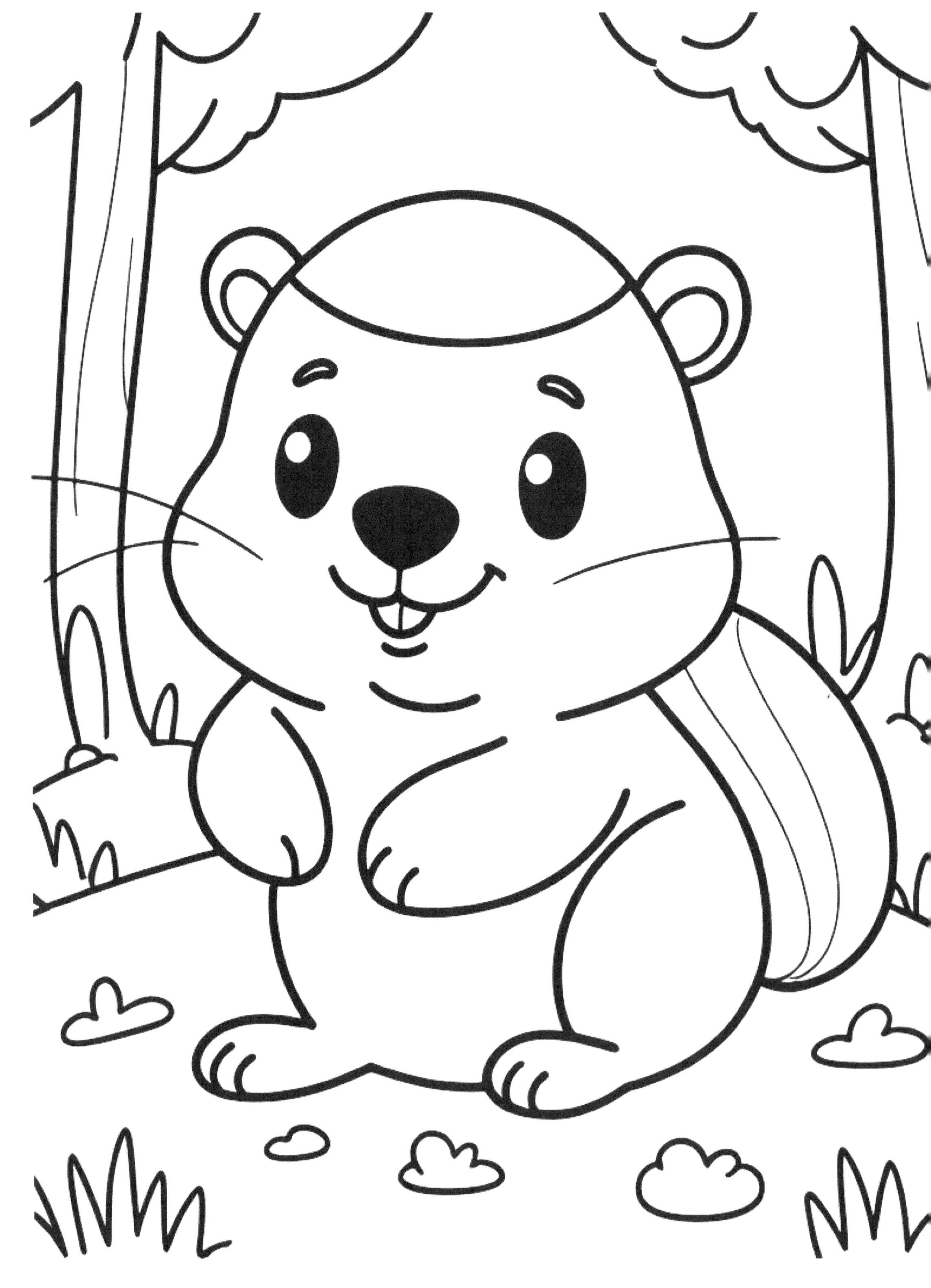

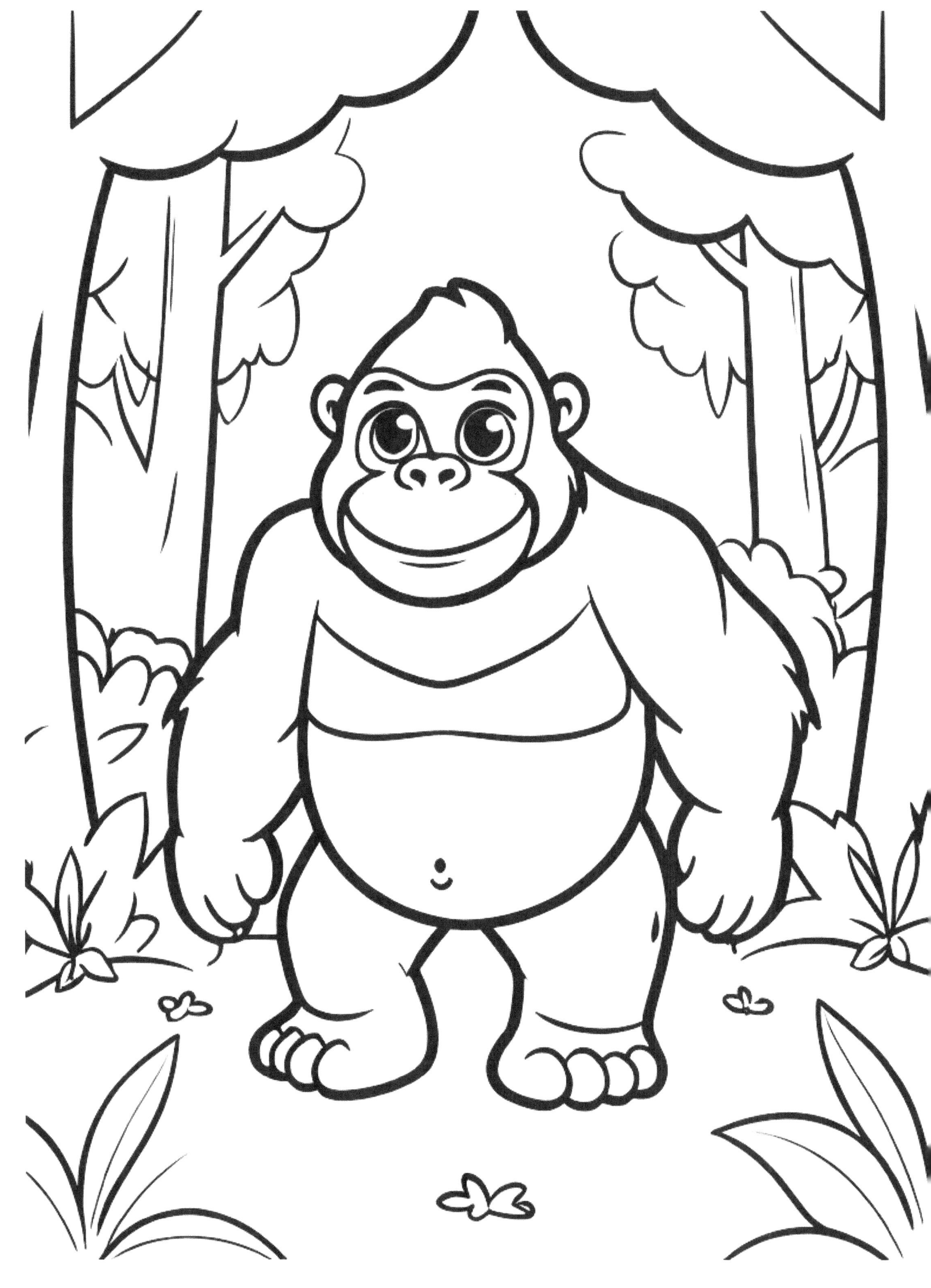

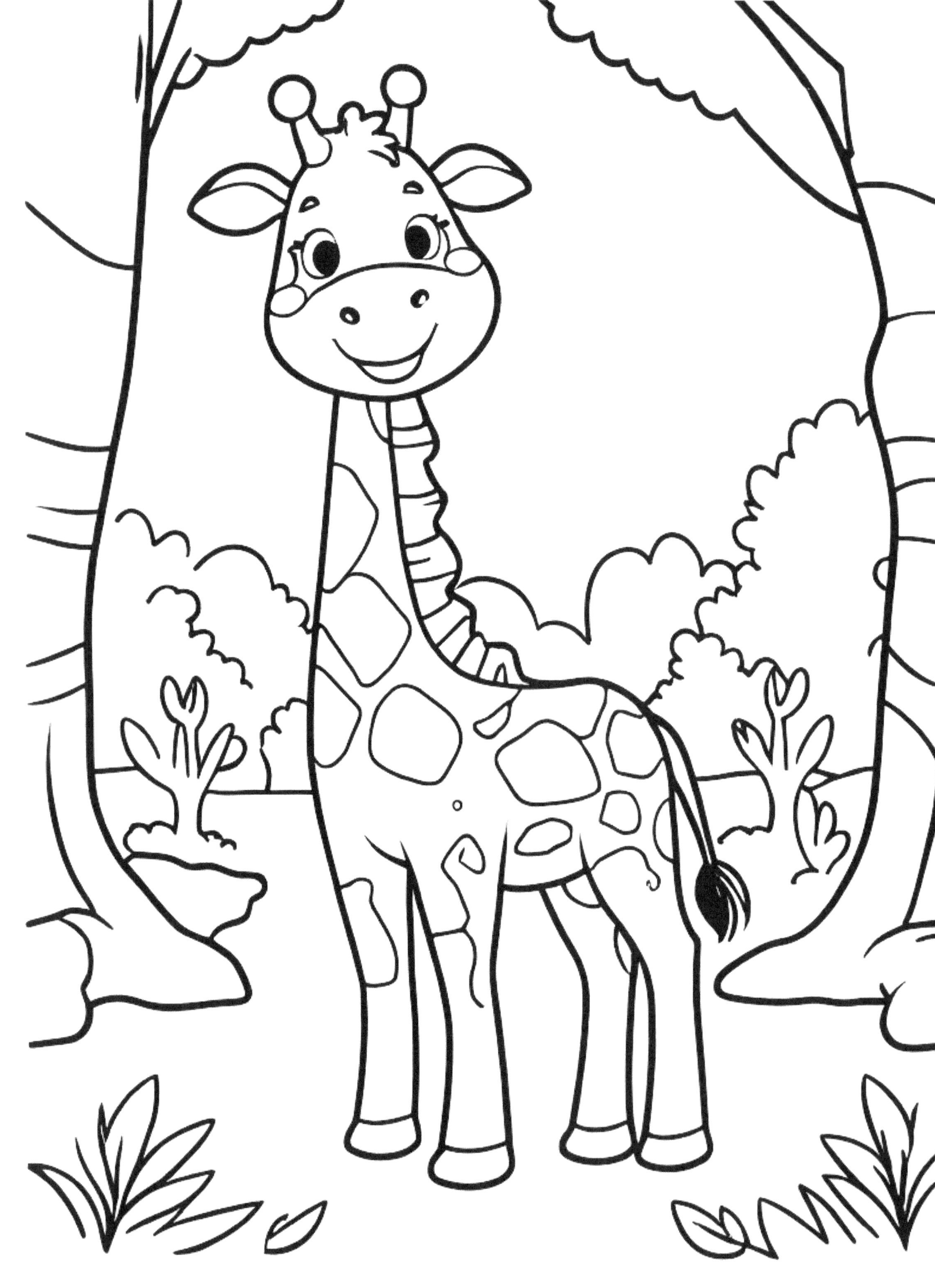

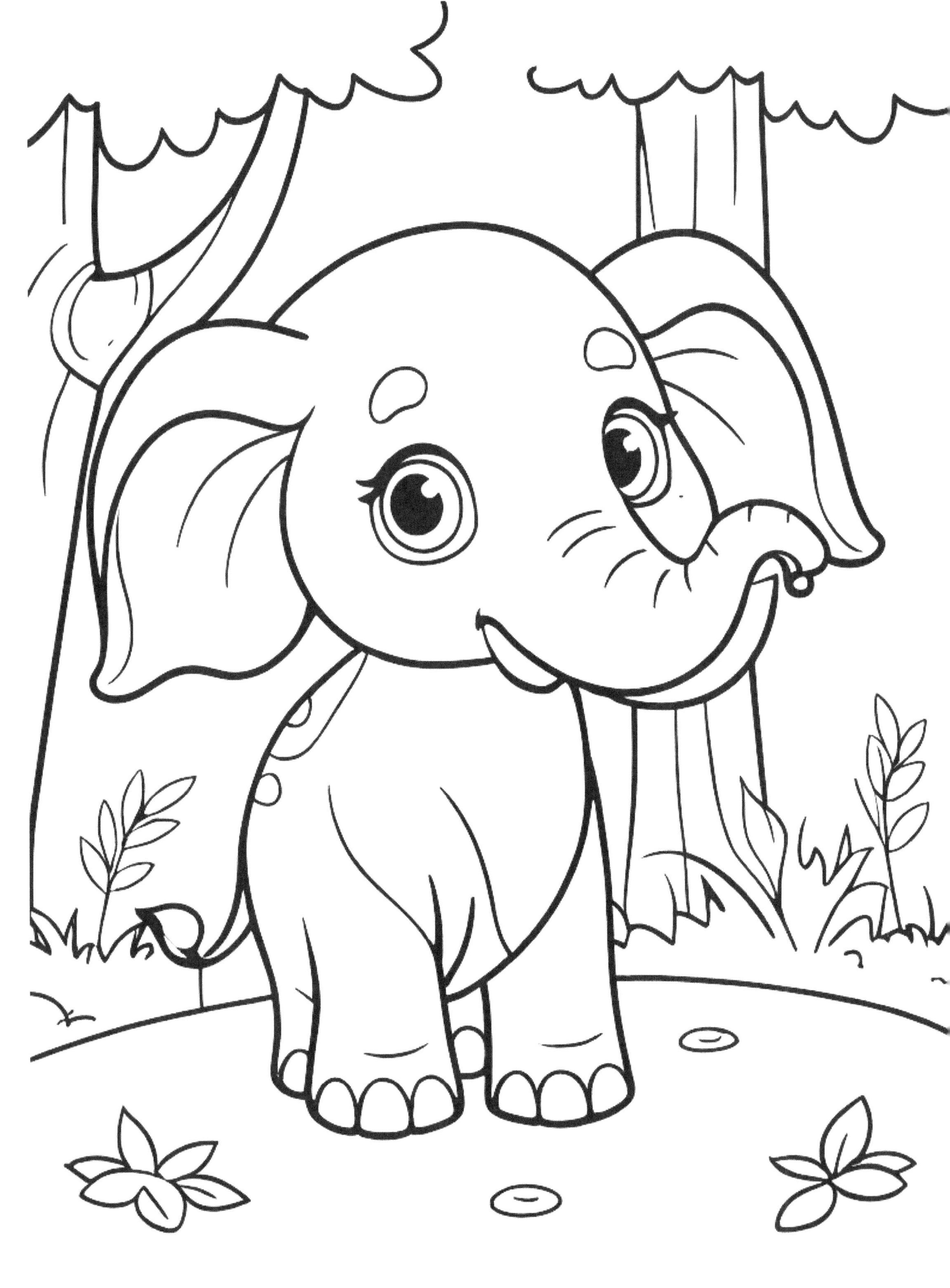

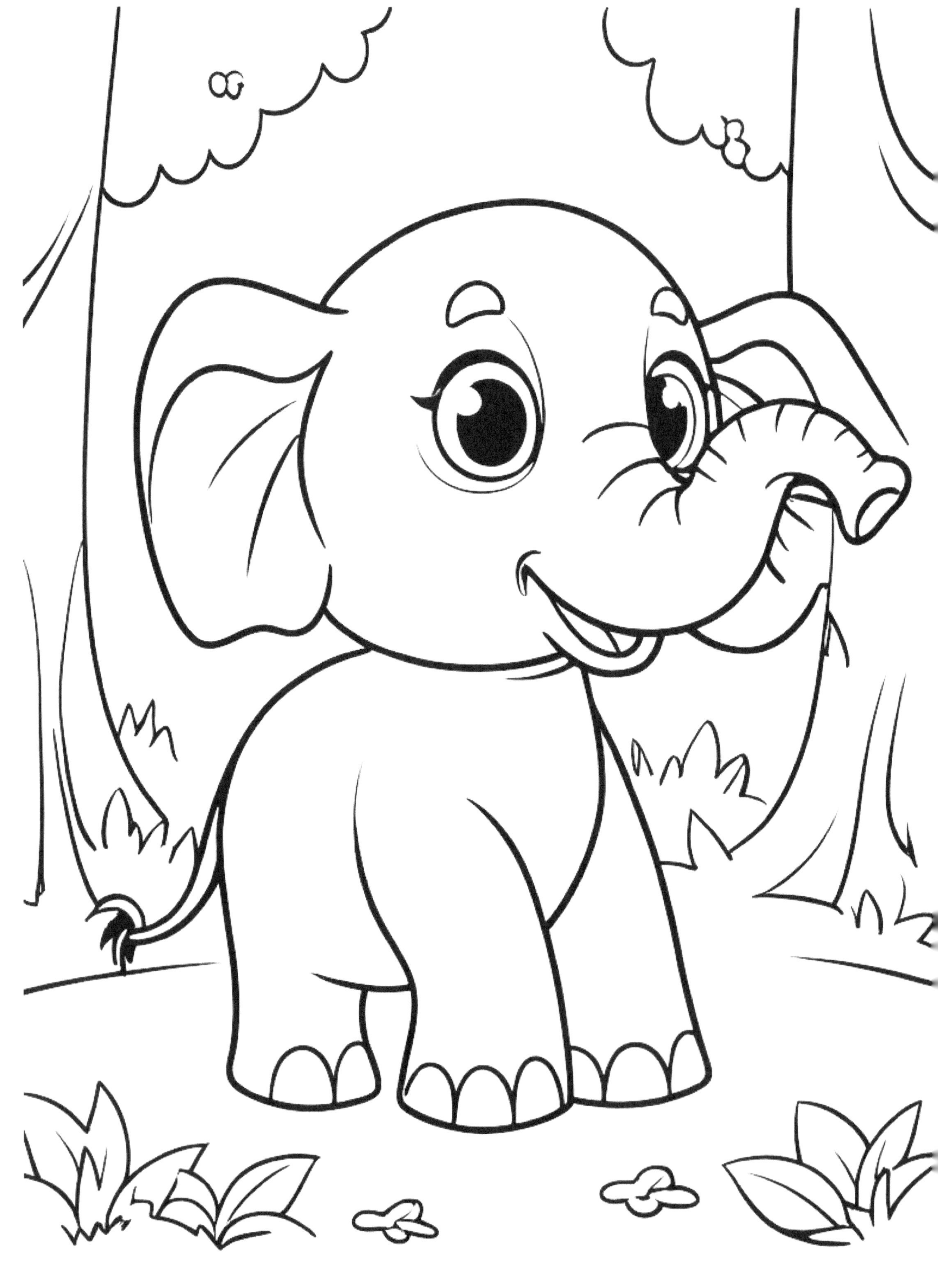

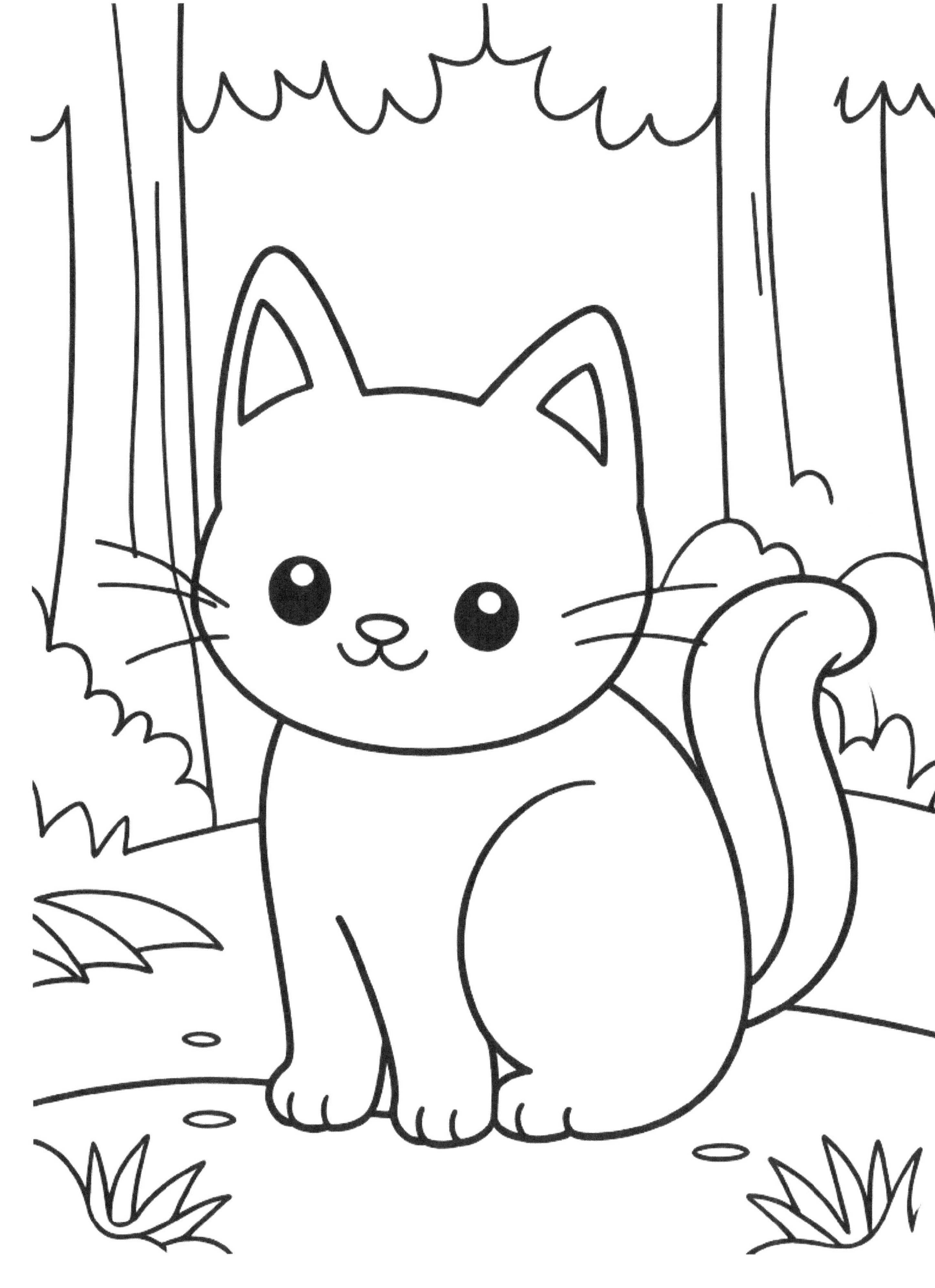

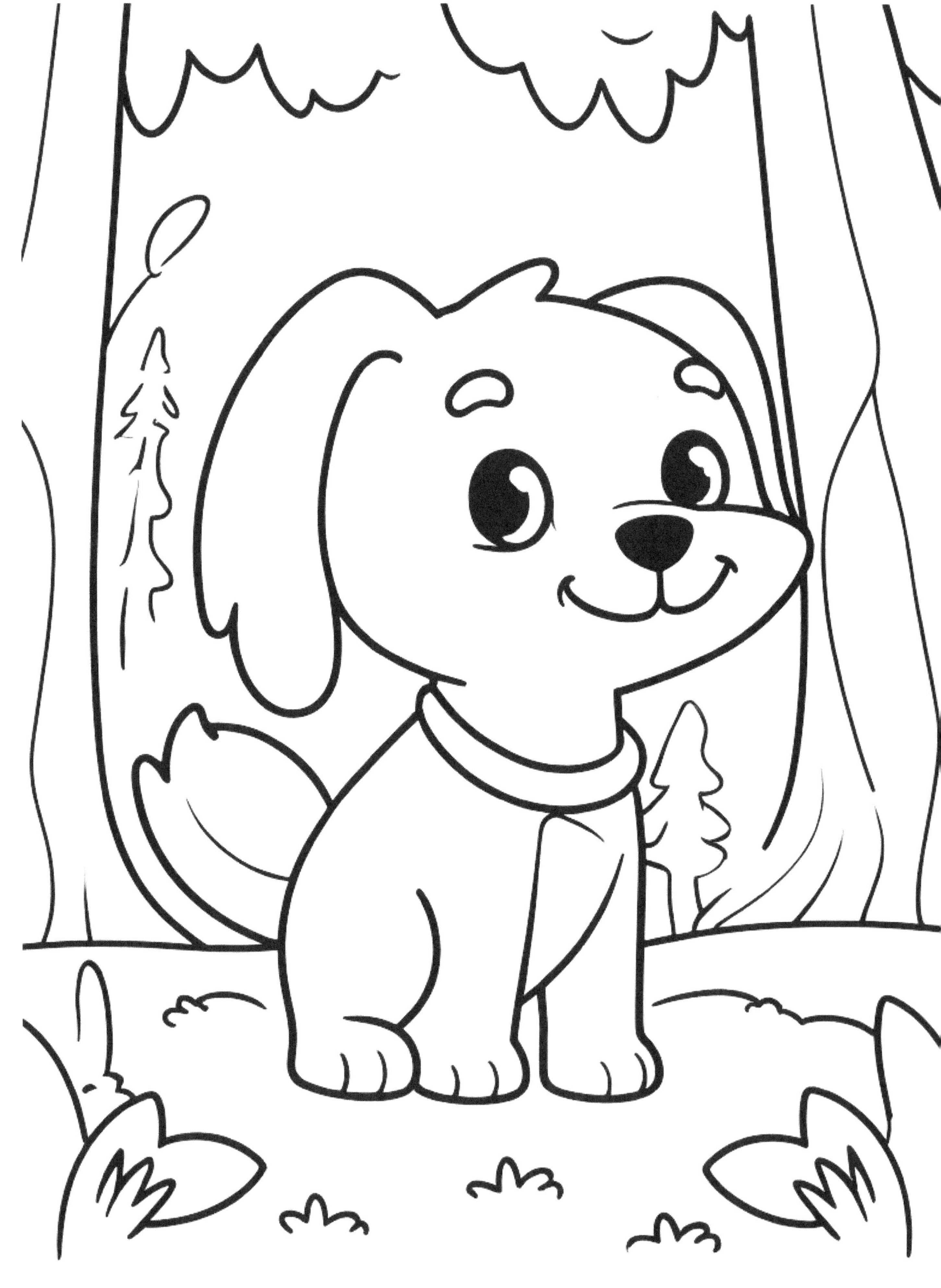

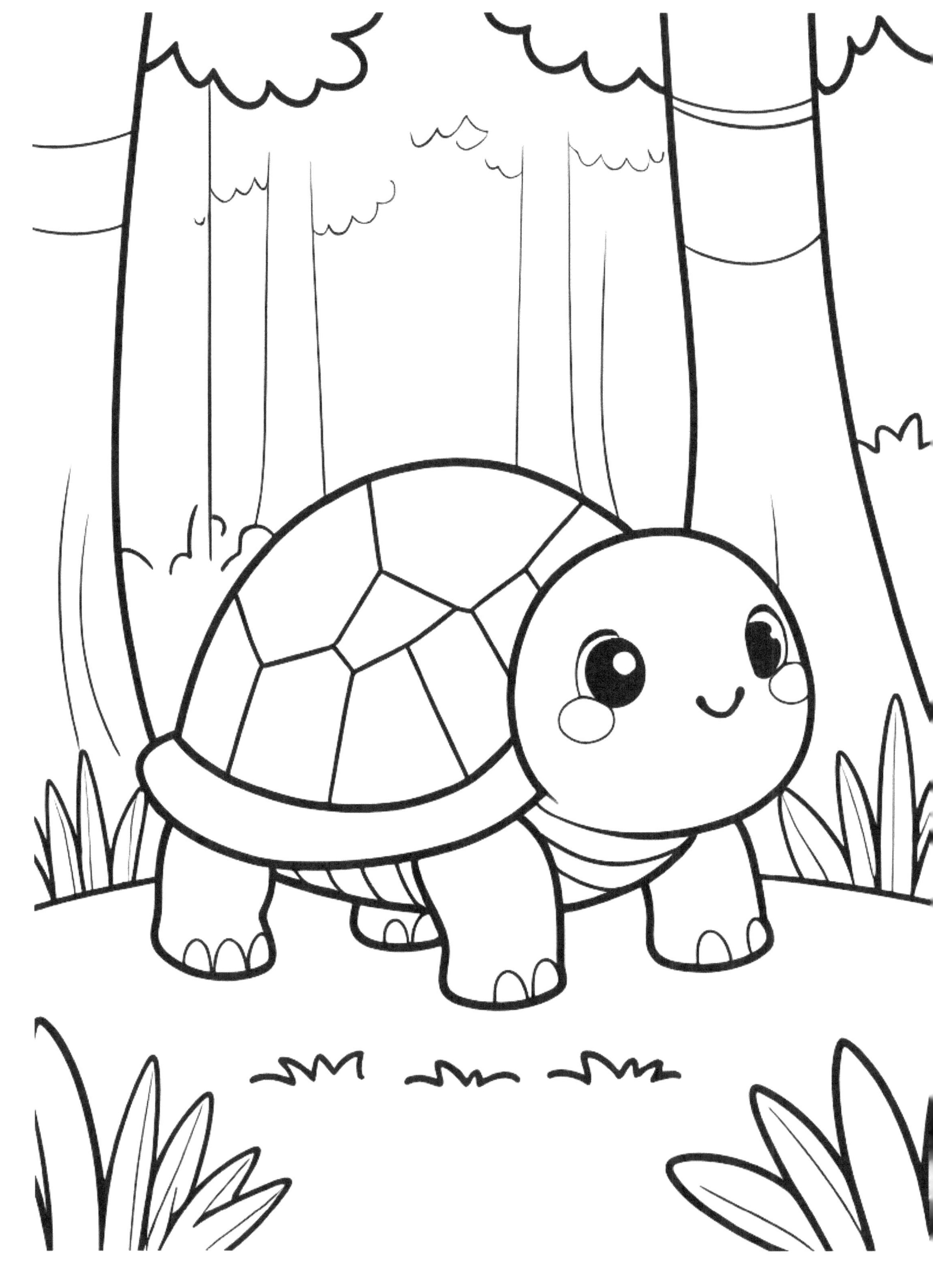

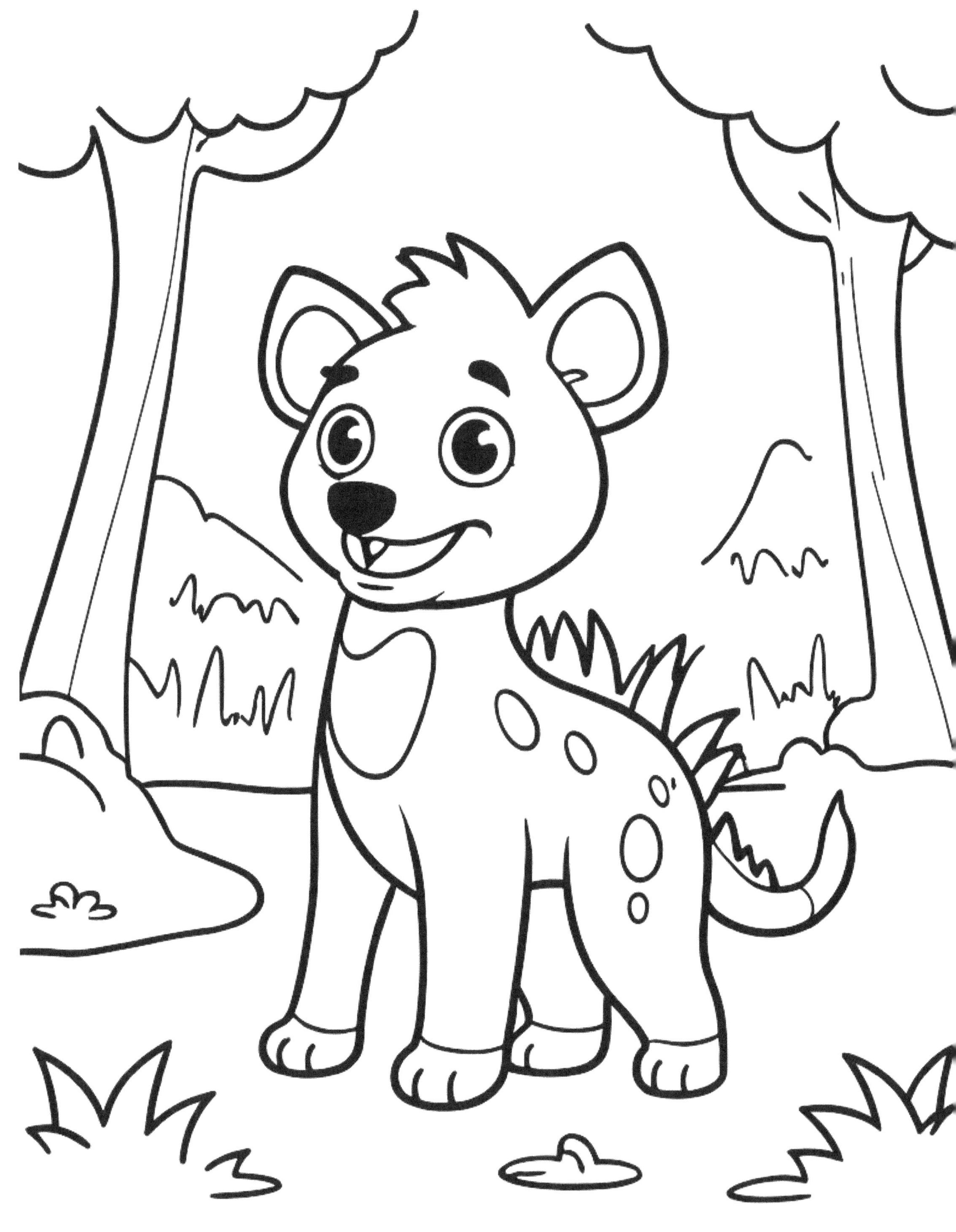

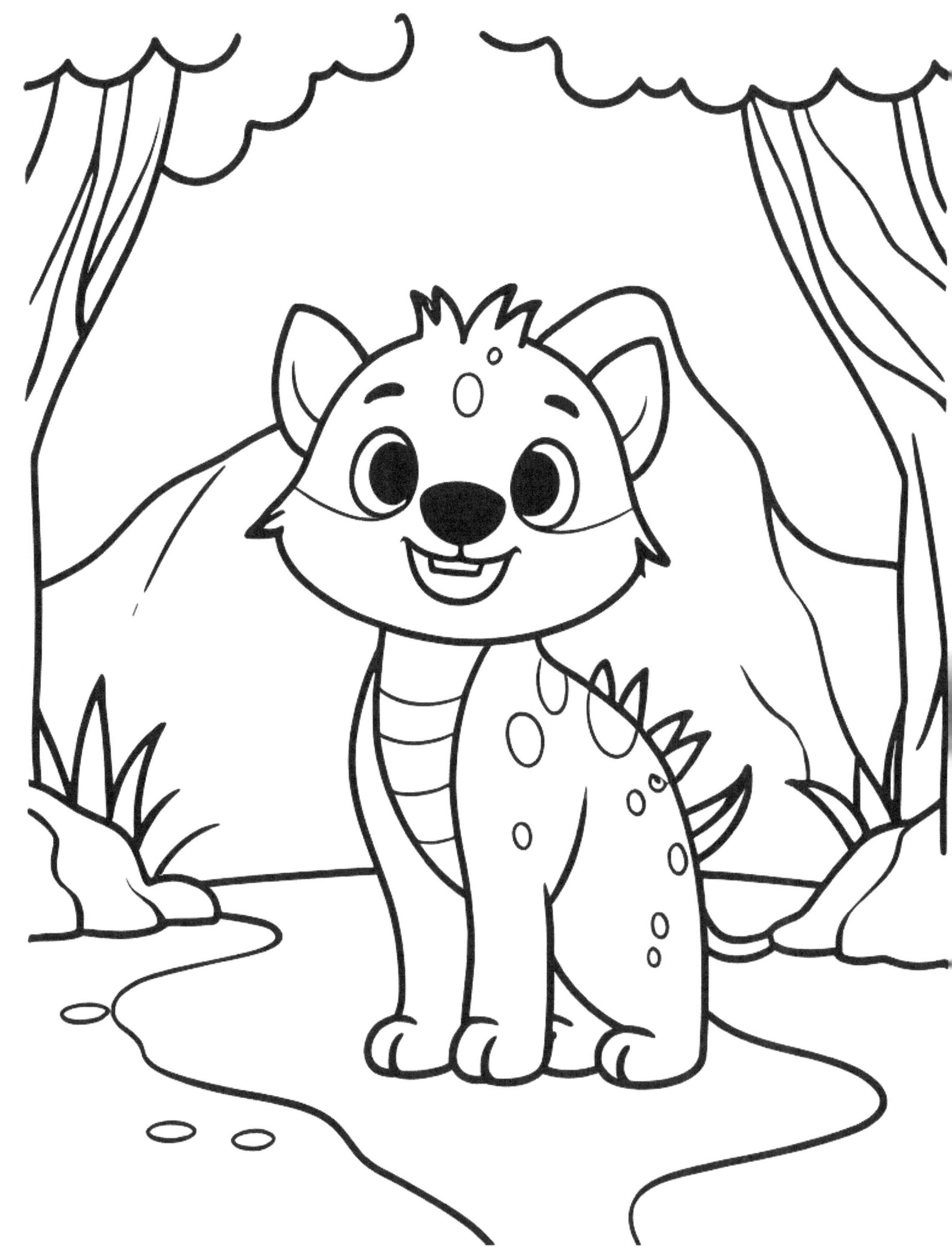

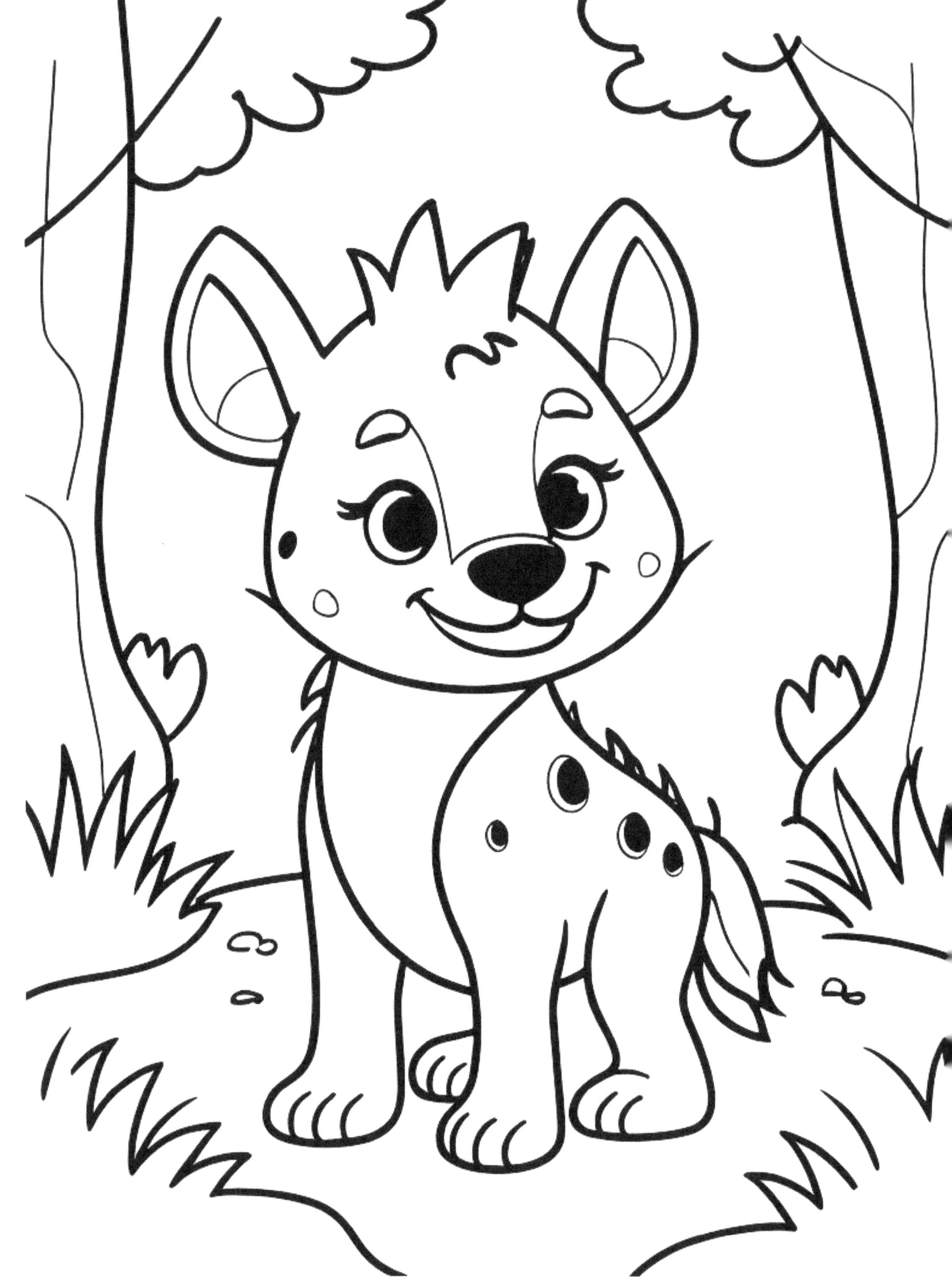

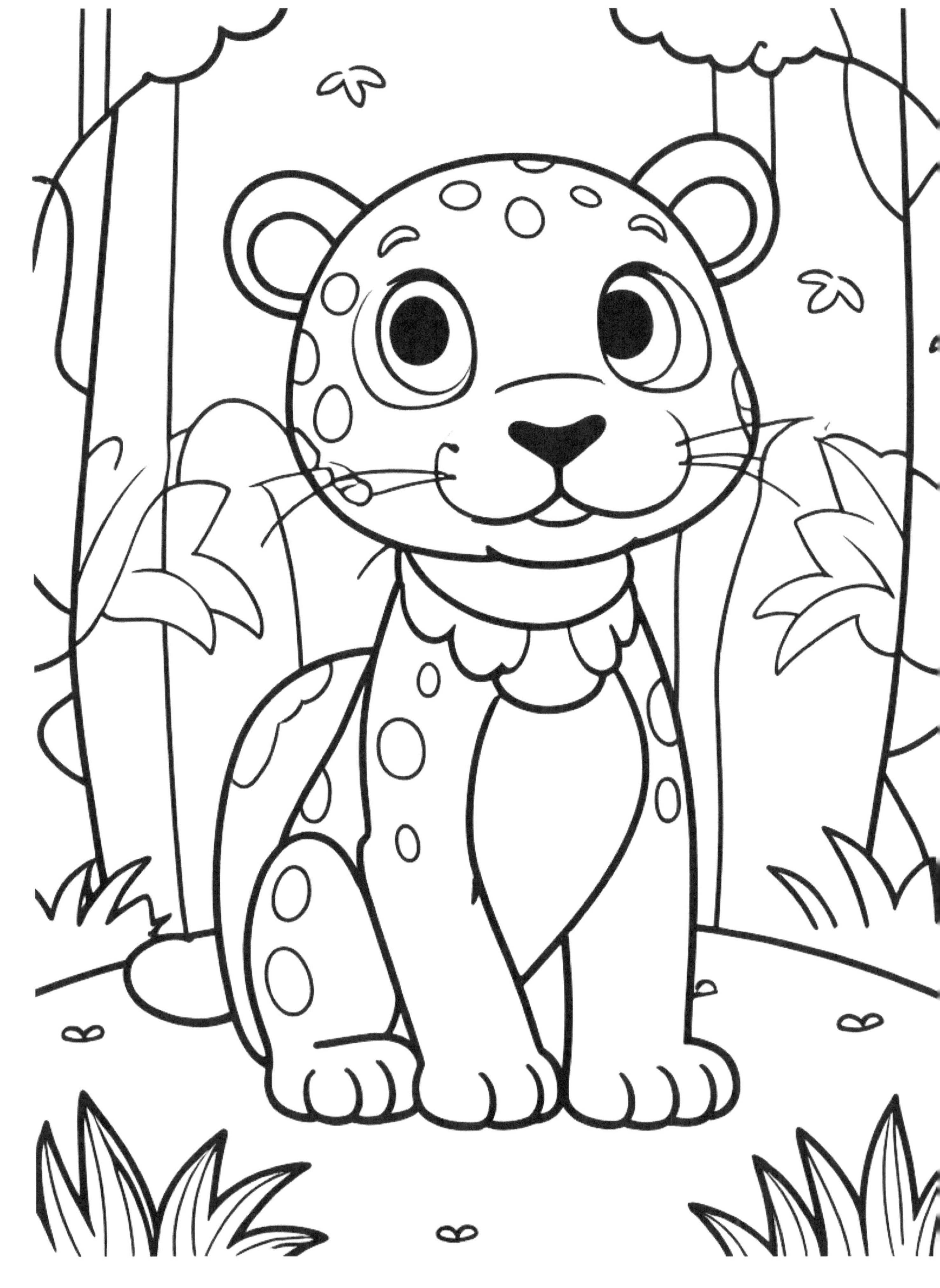

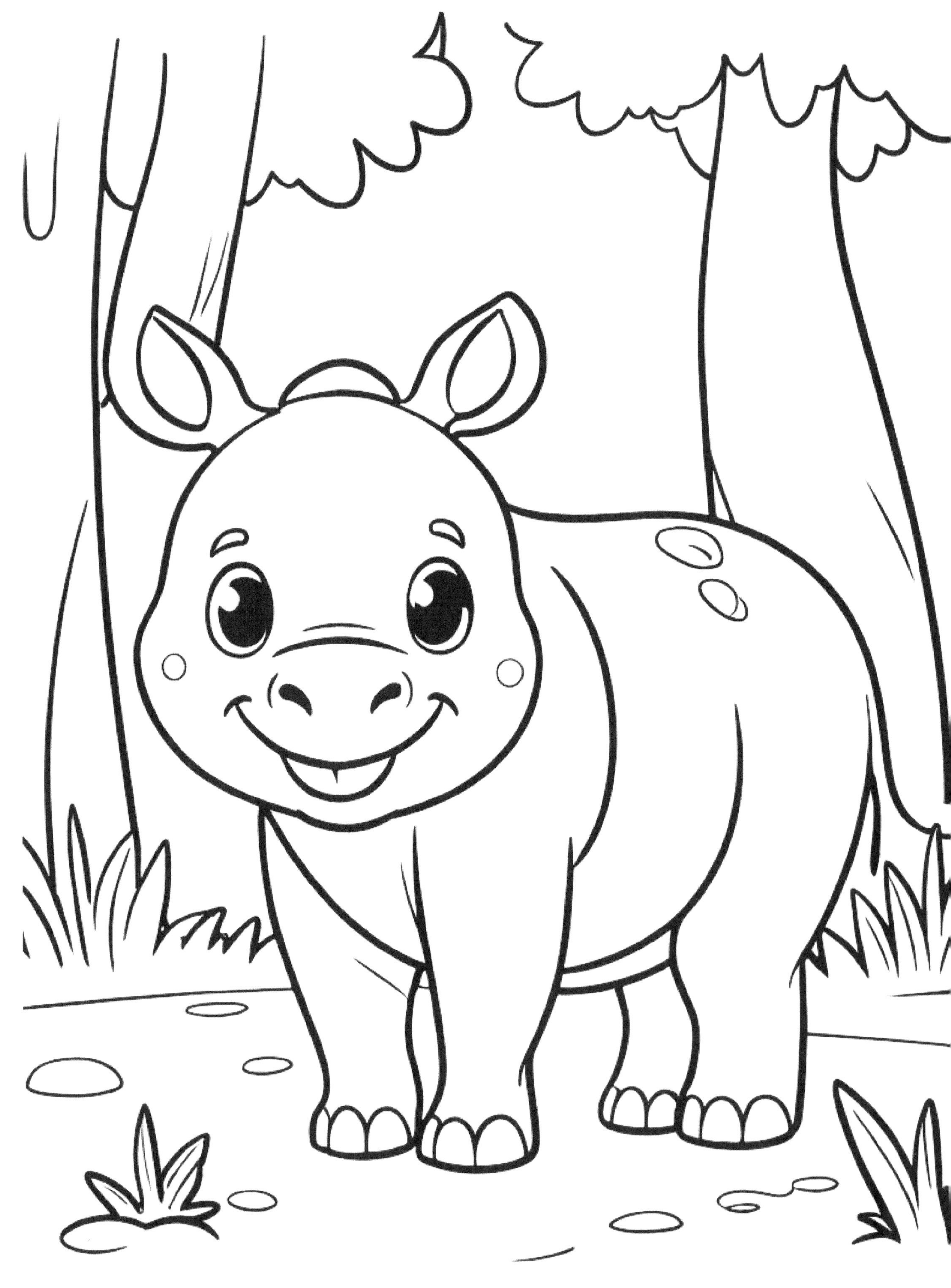

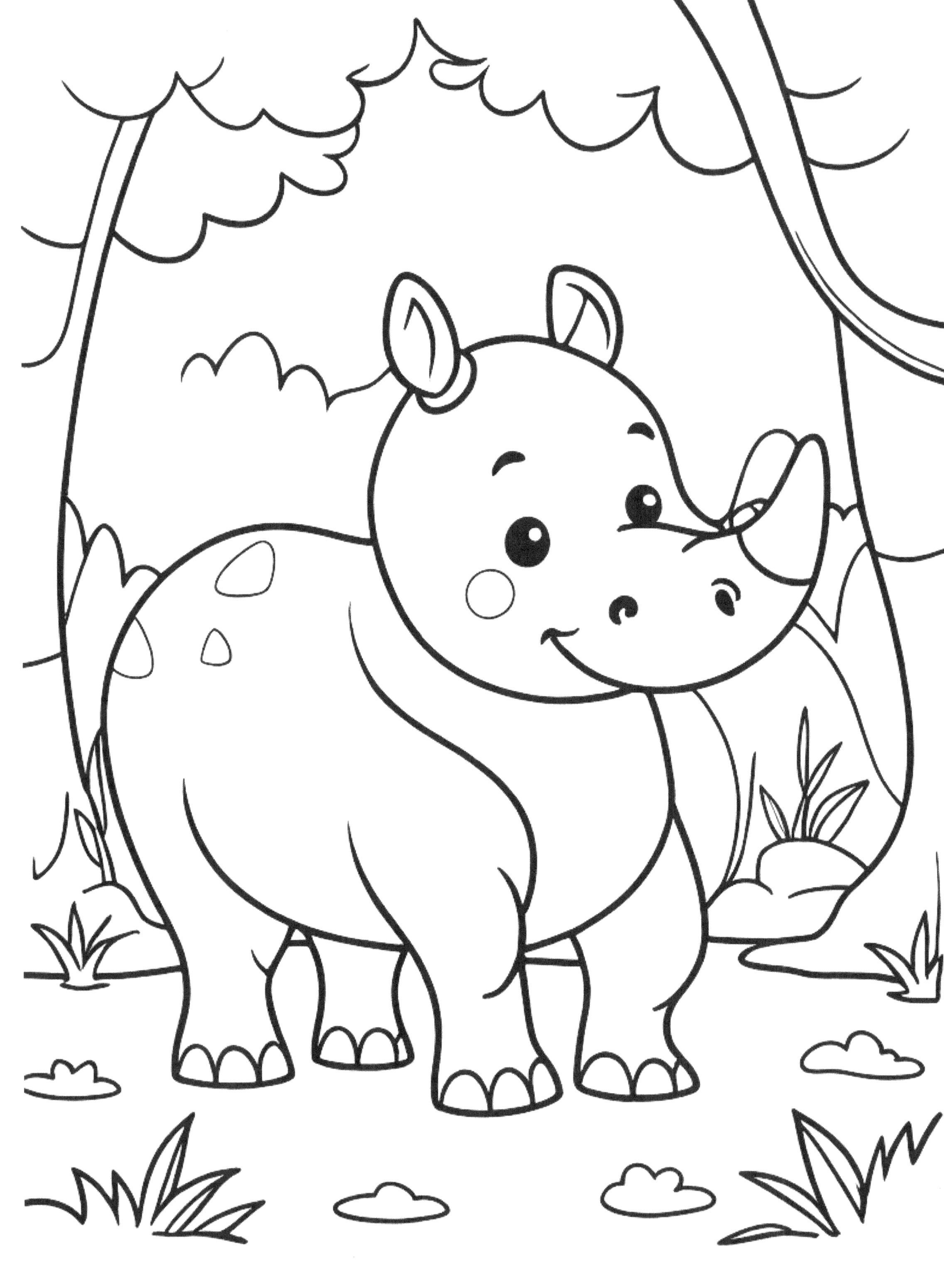

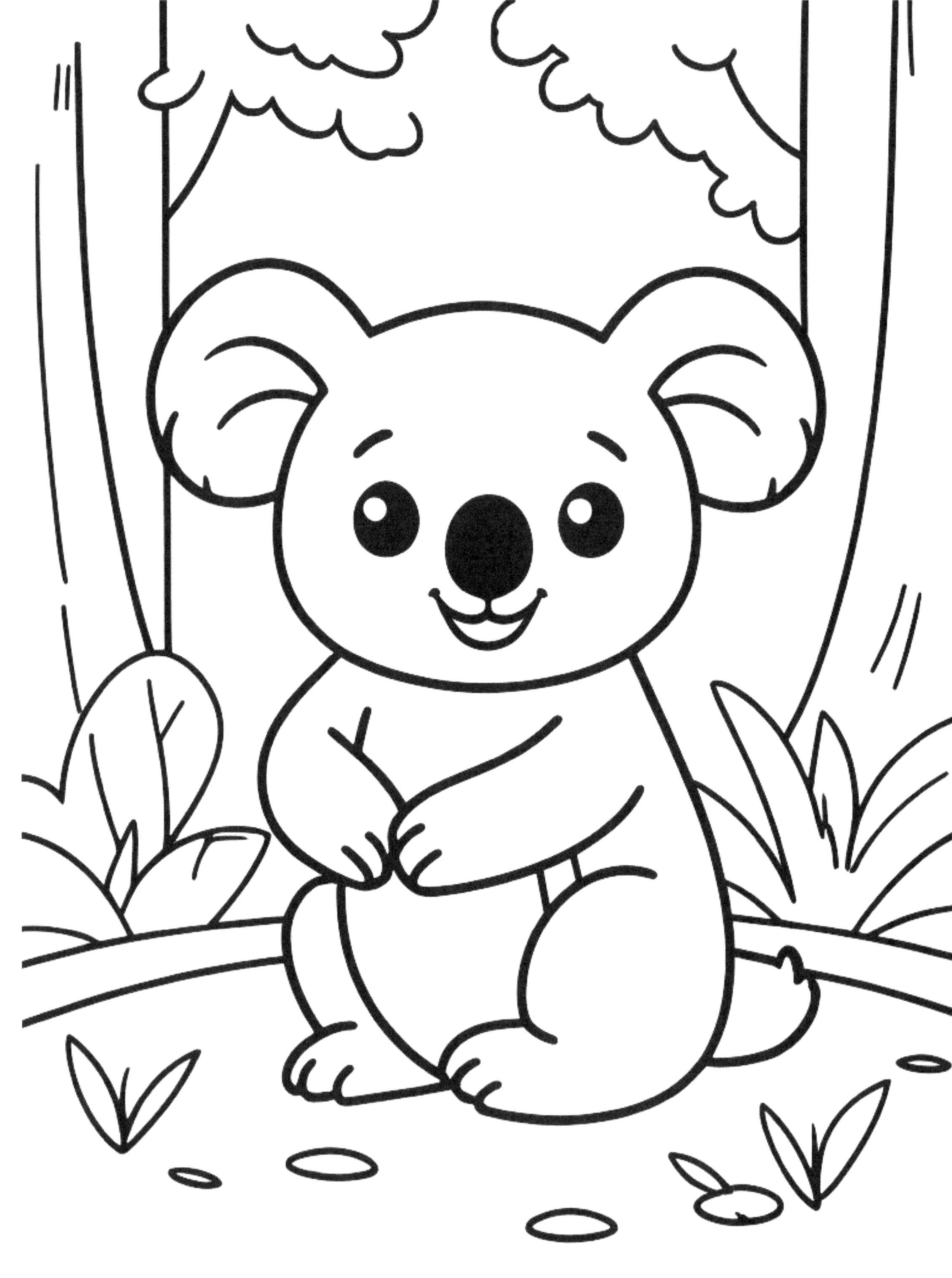

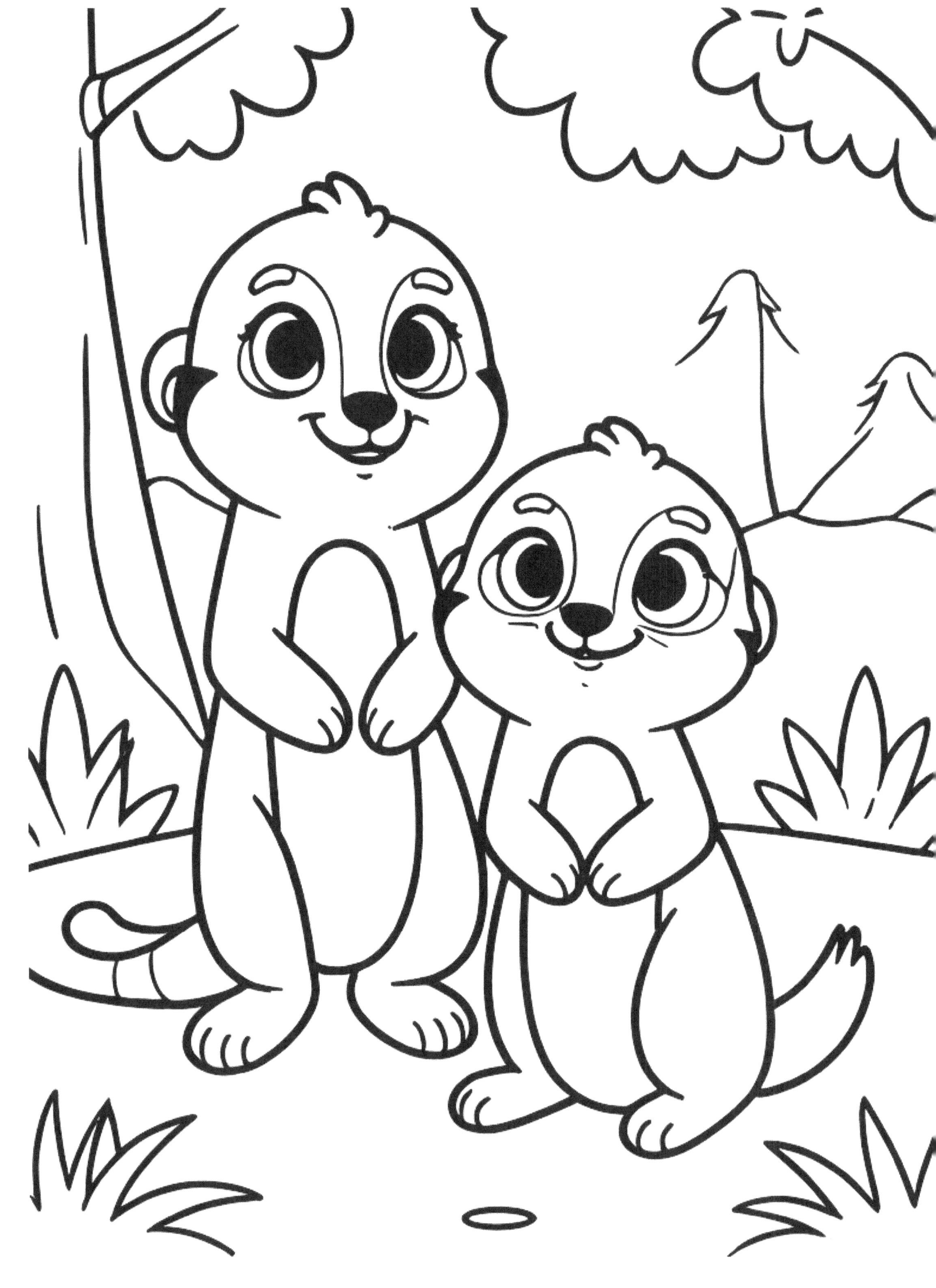

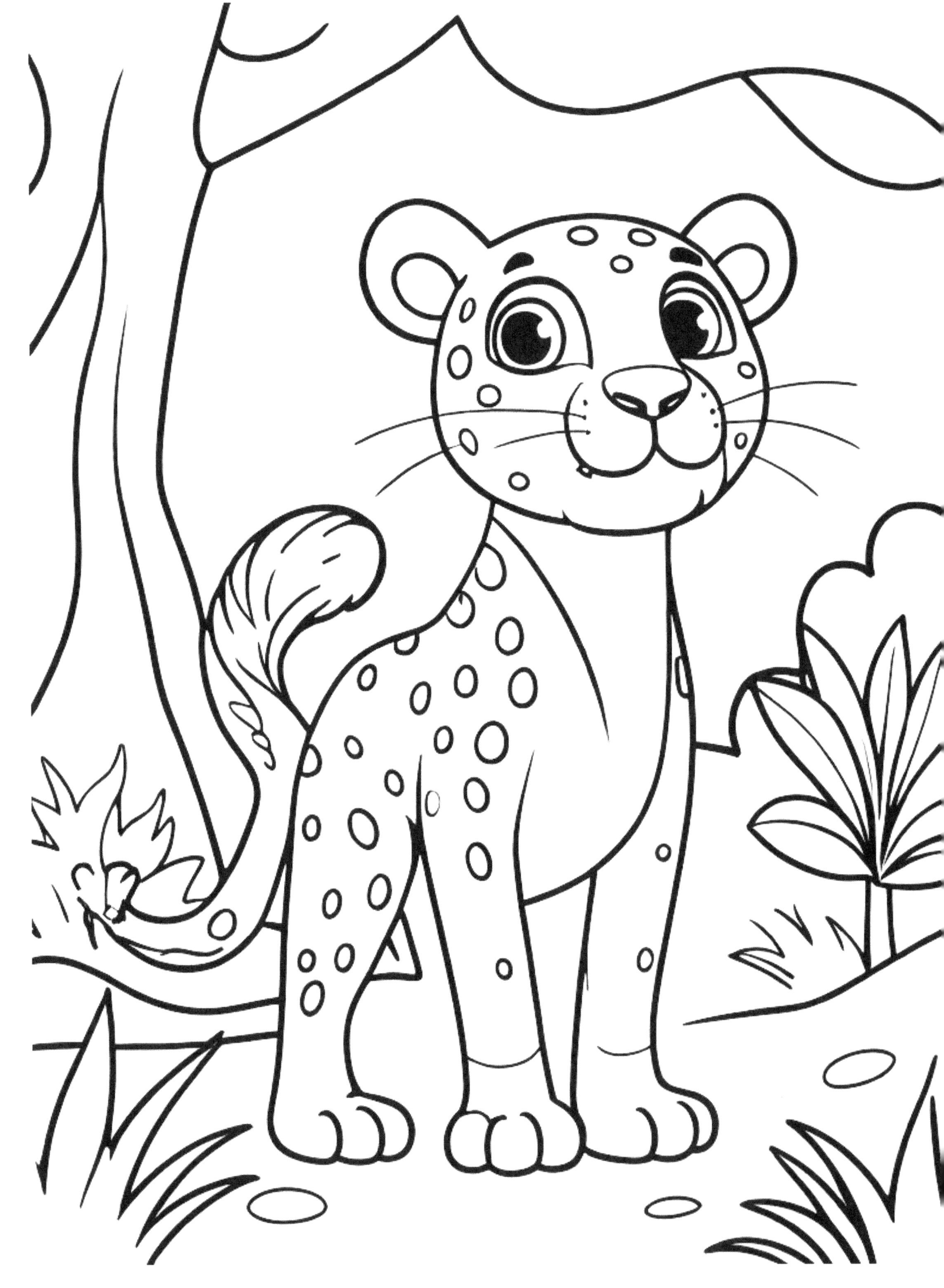

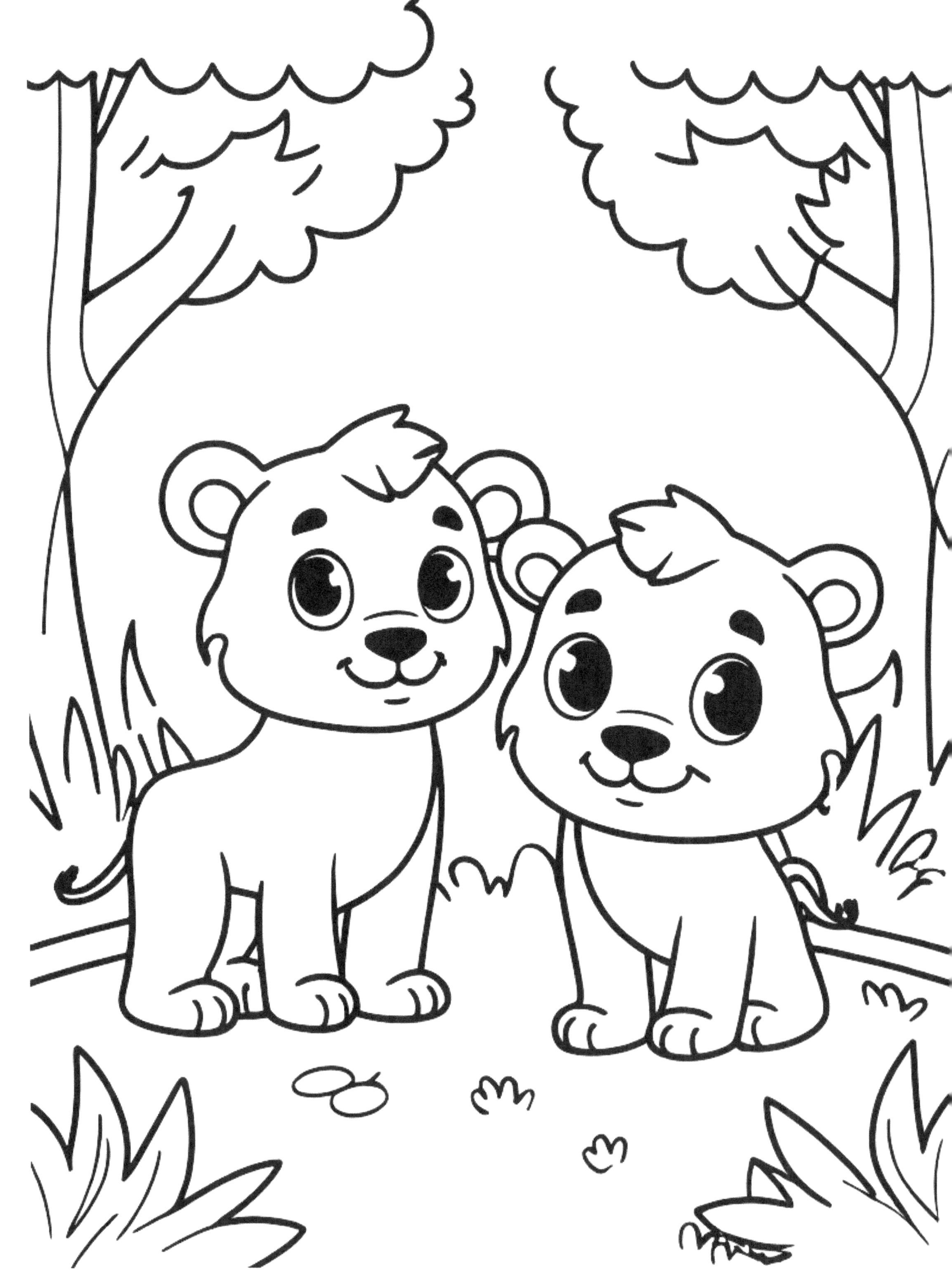

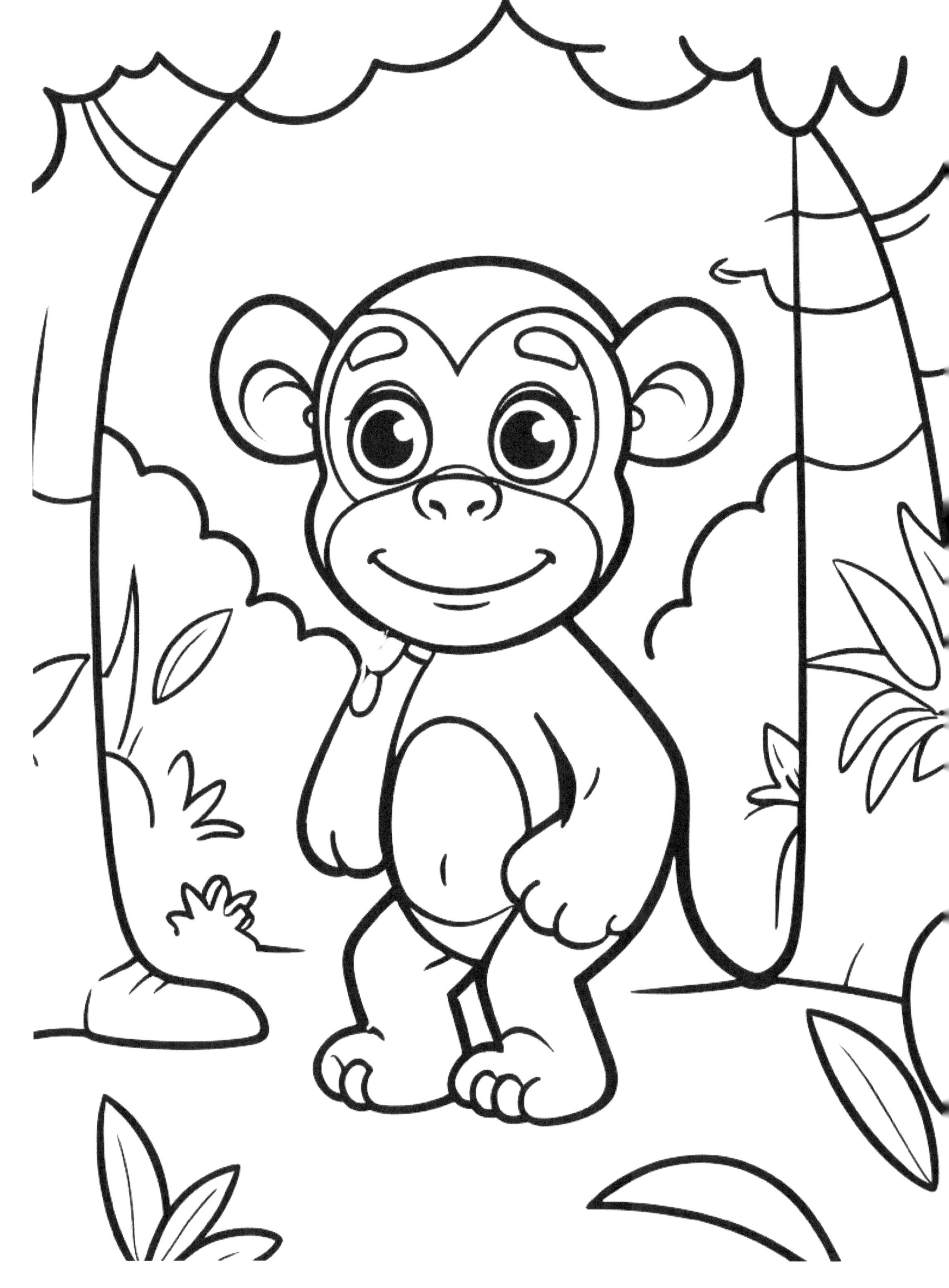

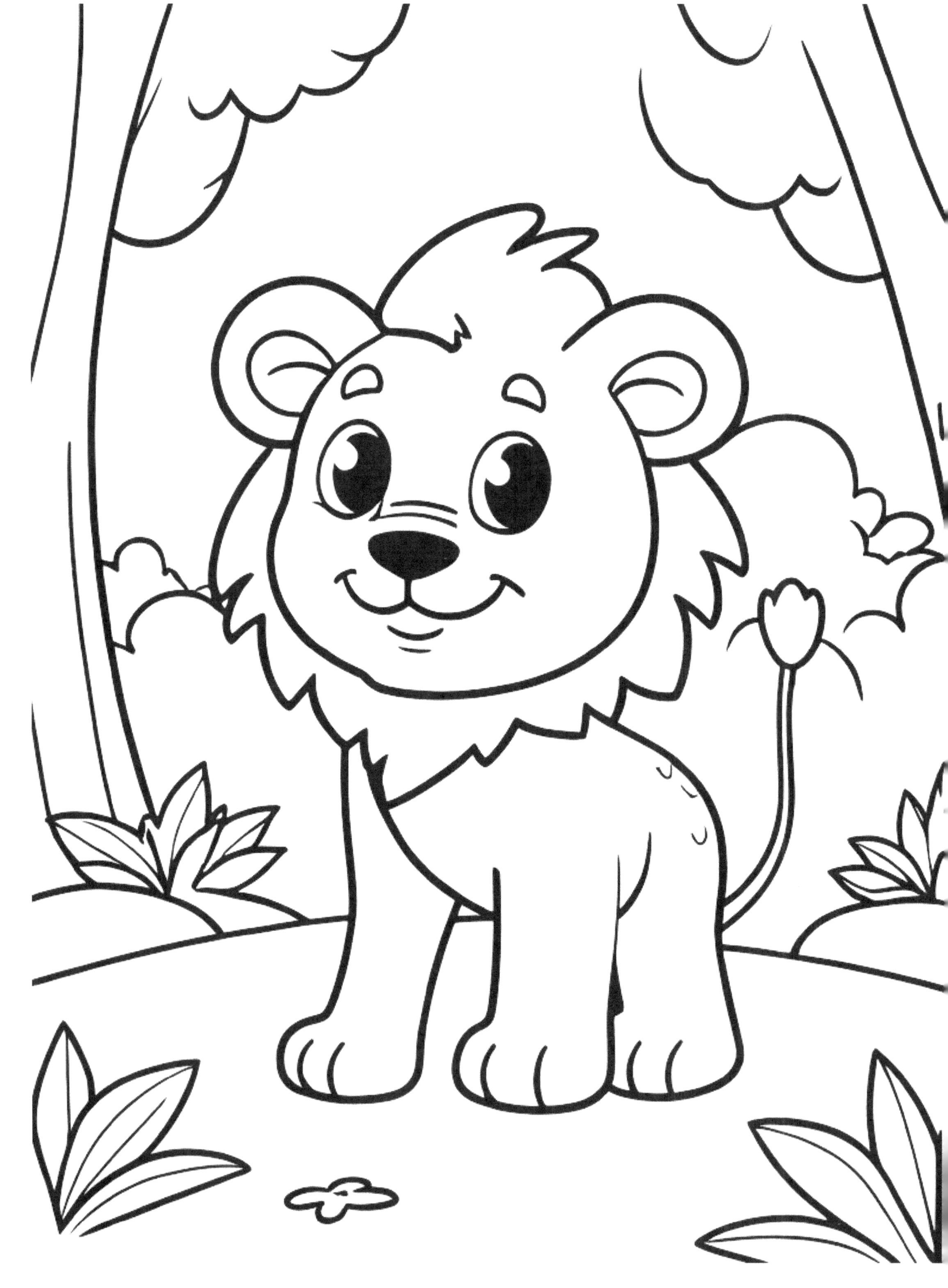

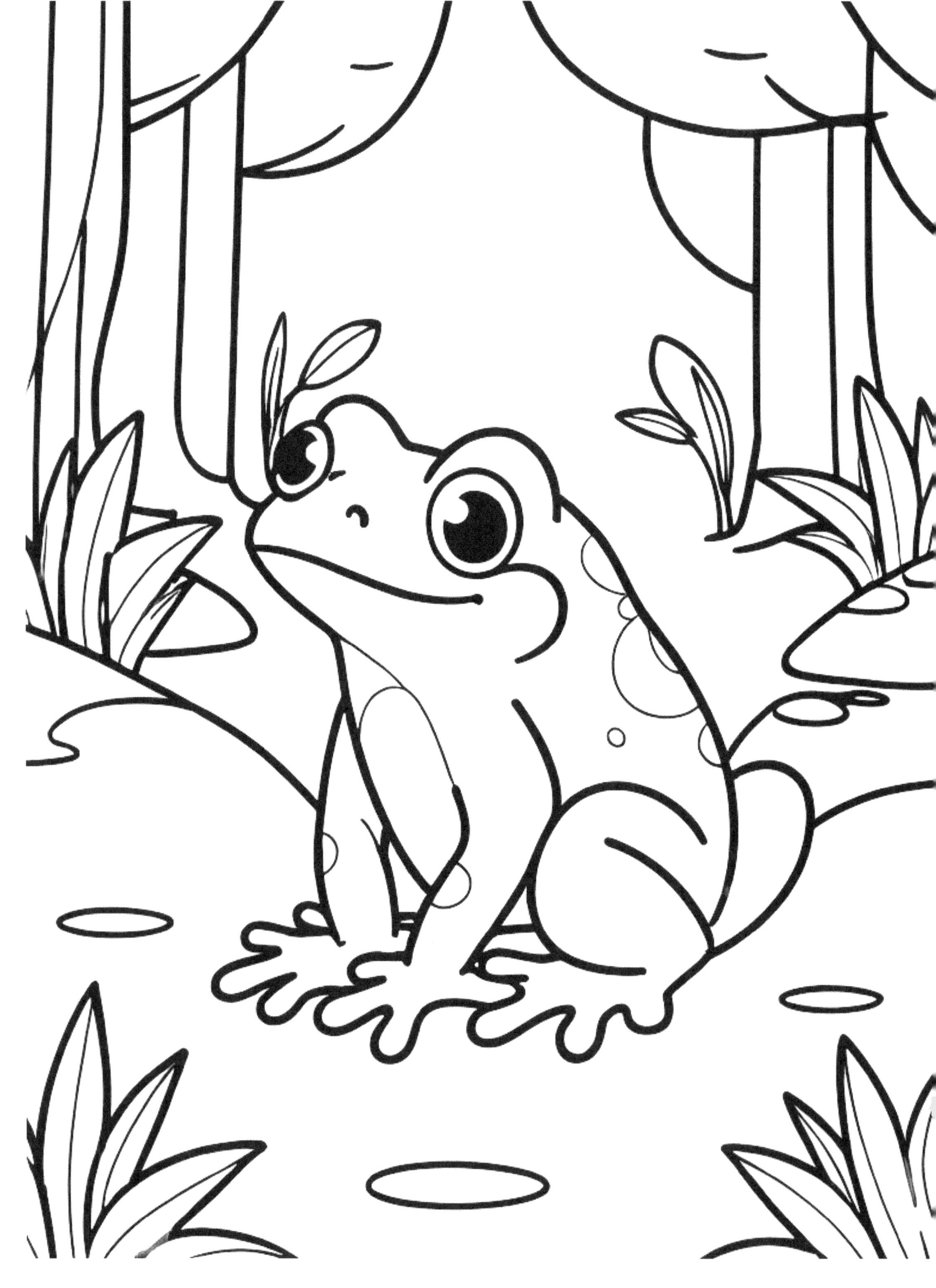